Dented

Sanchita Islam

CHIPMUNKA CLASSICS

Dented

CHIPMUNKA CLASSICS

Published by
Chipmunkapublishing
United Kingdom

http://www.chipmunkapublishing.com

ISBN   9781783823499

ARTS COUNCIL
ENGLAND

Chipmunkapublishing gratefully acknowledge the
support of Arts Council England.

FOREWORD

Written between 2007 and 2009 - the latter being the year of my first psychotic episode - this is Volume 2 of Dented, mainly comprising poems and prose. Unusually, I have decided to publish Volume 2 before Volume 1. Preferring to do things in reverse no one could ever say I was conventional, as an artist, writer, composer or human being. Rules are there to be broken, stamped on and trashed.

'Women are poetry', the late Leonard Cohen said; women were his muse, and his inspiration. Then what is mine?

- Unfathomable darkness
- The elusive moon
- The quivering line of the pen
- The safety of solitude
- The shallowness of beauty
- The random collision of colour
- The barbed wire edge of memory
- Shallow masks
- Scented flesh
- Futile obsession
- Lurid hues
- Incessant patterns
- A child's untarnished way of looking at the world
- The knowledge that something greater than man exists out there

Volume 2 deals with abstract topics and is more universal, perhaps. Volume 1 explores the themes of unrequited love, rejection, the dissection of mental and emotional pain.

Pain = Alchemy = Transformation

It is in Volume 2 that the mind makes a leap and transforms the pain into something other. There's a new poem written in November 2016, which I have included. It confronts the idea of a memory that haunts and crawls back to a single night in 2009 - the year my mind imploded. Why do negative memories linger and torment us? How can you be rid of them? The answer lies in acknowledging that man is weak and flawed; if you accept this you can forgive and move on without bitterness in your heart.

The idea of the tortured soul, the tormented artist, the one who is misunderstood by those that are close and the wider world in general, is a cliché. But this is my life, forever trying to find a place and in the end never quite fitting anywhere and being rejected because of my different brain.

Accepting that pain exists for a reason is comforting, perhaps I was meant to suffer in order to ameliorate the suffering of others.

The death of my father surfaces again and again in poems, since his absence created a profound dent in my heart and the subconscious mind - the dent of loss.

Many of these poems were written in minutes, like bullets shooting out of my head, fully formed - perhaps a residual effect of the manic state that I often find myself tossed about in. Mania is like dancing naked in the fire, if you can survive the heat, doors in your brain that remain closed for others fly open.

Revisiting this work has not been easy, I have made changes, edits and culled poems. Modifying, chipping and shifting, never quite satisfied, but you know when a poem is ready to be released into the world.

What I am trying to grasp at is a universal truth, even though truth doesn't exist and is a nebulous, slippery concept. Yet we all have an idea of what is real and matters and is important - a clumsy way of describing truth as I perceive and understand it to be.

During these years I was still working out the maze and insoluble puzzle that is the mind. It was through poems and prose that I began to identify patterns in behaviour that were directly linked with the sort of brain I possess. And we must remember that every brain is unique, there are

approximately seven billion of them out
there and rising - no one is the same. We
owe it to our wellbeing to try to fathom the
idiosyncrasies and strangeness that is our
own unique mental landscape.

I attempt to unravel it through music,
words and art.

Themes of love, illness, family, memory and
death flow like winding blue veins through
the poems.

Yet, I don't see myself as a poet, rather I
play with words and enjoy seeing them
dance on the page, stab people in the heart
and punch them in the gob.

Sanchita Islam

Clean

She cleans and cleans and cleans
Trying to scrape away every blemish and
smudge
Sometimes spending hours of her days
Scrubbing on hands and knees
Until they hurt
New marks appear like sores as the old
ones are banished
She frowns in dismay as she squeezes
chalky filler into the cracks
But they remerge like weeds
Only small ones
Barely detectable
But she can see them
As clear as a blue-sky day.
And then there is the accumulation of
useless possessions
'I vow to never buy anything again,' she
announces resolutely
She does not need more clothes, shoes,
handbags or books
'If only I could throw all this stuff away
and have nothing at all
One pair of shoes, one dress, one coat,
Just one of everything will do.'
She has boxes of receipts that make her
sick to the stomach
Another avaricious consumer
Gorging on *crap*
The crap builds up
Her whole existence is choked with clutter
Being truly naked without a single blemish
Is not possible

Perfection is a mug's game.
She visits her friends who happily live like
slobs
The dirt is brick thick
Their debris strewn everywhere proudly
The dishes piled high
They paddle in a luke warm sea of muck
with blissful indifference
And she envies their slothfulness
How many times can she fold a jumper?
How many times can she reorder a drawer?
How many times can she throw crap away?
Only to accumulate more
And more and more
Do these things compensate for what's
missing in her life?
Those kisses, those hugs, that dish of
tenderness
And sip of kindness
The food that she's been starved of
For years now
Does she think that order and cleanliness
Will mask the disorder of a sullied mind?
No real routine
No proper relationship
No children
Just this flat and all its peculiar contents
Draped in insidious layers of invisible grime
and stickiness
The muckiness of life
What would happen if her exterior world
mirrored her interior one?
What would that world look like?
A jungle of mayhem,
An installation occupying every corner

Surfaces steeped in stuff
So dense
Merging with her own skin
Impossible to scrub clean.

The Ignominious Mouse

A gentle breeze blowing against her tired
face was the closest the skinny one
Would ever get to intimacy that day
As she wandered into a café
In search of a quick sugary fix
A blue-eyed blond sat opposite glued to a
screen
People comatose, stitched to their
computers all over London
Doing what?
Distracting minds
A temporary diversion
From the errant details that
Complicate all our lives
Her psychotherapist said, 'You have to
resolve the conflict within'.
The conflict
What was that exactly?
Not to want or need versus the desire to
want or need
'It's irresolvable,' she muttered to herself
The birds were singing, their chorus
incessant and vexing
As she worked aimlessly in early morning
darkness
Then in the corner of her eye a murky, grey
shadowy figure
Tried to sneak past the plant pot
Disturbing her previously chilled repose.
She leapt from her bed,
Gasping as if besieged
Was she afraid of the offender,
Violated that an uninvited guest had

invaded her space?
Like the soldier who enters a home at night,
Pointing a gun in a girl's face as she
trembles in her vest and knickers.
Right then she was lost, not knowing what
to do
Would she be able to resolve the issue of an
intrusive mouse?
She wanted someone to help her
To rescue her from that menacing rodent
She was tired and craved for her bedroom
to be the safe haven that it no longer was
A place where she could sleep
Snug and safe each night
Cut off from everyone and everything that
was scary in the world.
Too much of a coward to confront the
mouse
Terrified she was
No sleep came that night.
The mouse, too, was in a panic
Suddenly exposed,
Danger was imminent,
But there was no safe place to escape to
This room was its prison as the mouse
awaited its fate.
How many days had it been skulking in dark
corners as she slept?
Stupidly oblivious
Perhaps there was a whole family having
parties in her living room,
Shadows skimming past her nose,
Mouse droppings deposited in her Gucci
shoes.
She did not try to reason with the mouse,

There was no negotiation,
Simply she called in pest control to
eliminate the furry thing.
The mouse tried desperately to escape
Knowing it shouldn't have ventured into
unknown territory
In search of crumbs and stale morsels to
eat.
A huge man with a menacing stick was hell
bent on pulverising it
The mouse ran with fierce alacrity,
But there was nowhere to hide and the
skinny one was impatient for an end.
The little mouse began to shit with fear,
The tiny droppings were everywhere
And hardly unpleasant
She could have opened the door
Let the poor thing out
It was just an innocuous mouse
Hardly an ignominious intruder.
Before she could say, 'Don't kill it'
The mouse was battered to death,
A white plastic bag its coffin,
Its body a soft, grey diminutive mass
She felt a tinge of guilt,
But then other mice might crawl up pipes
and snuggle up beside her
There would always be others.
Was the solution swift elimination or
toleration?
The same could not be said of people
She couldn't batter people to death and
dump them in the river Thames
If they irked her
Then again if someone was unpleasant or

unkind
She could always walk away
Close the door
Cut them out
Flush her phone down the toilet
Throw her computer out the window
Cut off her tongue
Gouge out her eyes
Swap her brain for another
Emigrate
Murder the memory just as she murdered
the mouse.

The Heart

'What does it feel like when your heart is hurting?'
'In pain,' the skinny one thought long and hard about the concept
'If someone stamps on my heart
They jump up and down until it's no longer pumping and
Flat like paper
Then they cut it up into tiny pieces with very sharp scissors
Throw the fragments into a blender
Mix in some bleach
Listen to the sizzle and
Pour the pitiable concoction down the sink
Turn on the tap until
All trace of my heart is gone.
Afterwards I have to regrow my heart from scratch,
It always grows back eventually.
Often it takes a considerable amount of time and coaxing
To persuade the heart to return to the world;
The heart is fearful of another terrifying ordeal
And is reluctant to grow back to its full size.
The heart surmises that if it stays small
No one will notice it anymore
This is why re-growing a heart is such an arduous process.
I've lost count how many times I've had to regrow my heart
It is a very tiny, unobtrusive thing now

My heart beats slowly
Barely audible
Hardly visible
A little softer
A littler redder
But perfectly formed and tiny
Incredibly potent and sensitive
Despite its puniness
This is how I would describe my heart.'

The Painting

Every day is a blank canvas
Every day is a new painting

A fairly wise man asked the skinny one,
'What do you need when you paint?'
'Patience,' the skinny one replied without
thinking
And then he asked,
'What kind of painting will your day be
today,
A bright sunny one
Dark
Dull
Or blank?'
How daunting a prospect to determine the
brush strokes that make each day of life.
Some days perhaps the skinny one was not
sure what to paint
Preferring to leave the canvas toothpaste
white.
And what if each relationship resembled a
painting?
And each word she uttered was a brush
stroke?
Her life was strewn with discarded
paintings,
Doomed friendships and futile love affairs.
When she tried to visualise these disastrous
paintings
They were chaotic
Abysmal attempts at abstract expressionism
Often executed with her eyes closed
She stamped on her paintings

Cutting up big chunks of canvas
Throwing handfuls of paint with tense fists
All emotion and anger
Impetuous and irrational
Without a single, deft touch
Resulting in a gooey catastrophe.
She didn't want to retrieve all these awful
paintings
They were in a large skip now
Somewhere at the back of her mind
Forgotten junk.
Now when she met someone
She thought carefully about that first critical
brush stroke
The colour, the shade and the type of
painting she wished to make.
'I will create intricate oil paintings,' she
decided
With the finest sable brushes
But was everyone a meticulous oil painting?
she wondered
Some people would remain colossal,
monstrous, abstract paintings
With lurid colours and textures and bumps,
Others were morose, monochrome
paintings,
While the rest were saccharine scenes
painted in sickly, colours.
Occasionally there would be a painting that
defied all expectations
Like a Rauschenberg that was playful and
clever
With a moose head protruding from its
canvas heart.
Some tried to intervene and

Steer her brush in another direction.
When alone no one controlled her brush,
Only the skinny one could wield it in a
solitary dance
On an expanse of white
She would trust herself to know which
colours to mix
And where to nudge or let it be
She knew that it was possible to create
magic with her fingers.
Memories of failed canvases
Would encroach and inhibit the skinny one
from
Picking up a brush and making
The timid strokes that were
The first conversation
The subtle colours that became
The gentle touch
The grand compositions that would evolve
over time
Into something remarkable and
Quite unique
With amorphous bits that were
Unfathomable.
And the surface shifted from gold, to silver,
to ultramarine blue to blood red with a
streak of ochre
And when you scrutinised the painting
critically
It didn't matter whether you comprehended
the marks
That made up the painting
If you felt compelled to stare a little longer
At the crust that was its very skin
Then the painting was alive

And breathing in the world;
These were the paintings that
Made up life.

'What will I paint today?' the skinny one
asked.

Existence

The birds were singing on this first sticky
night of summer.
As her eyes flickered
Half awake
Half asleep
She thought about existence:

The man working in a sweatshop in India
From dawn to dusk
Each garment brings in a few rupees,
My life is worth nothing, he thought as he
sewed
Earning just about enough to eat,
To clothe his children and feed his wife
To live in a rat infested slum
Where the air stank of shit
His life was hand to mouth
Short and brutal
Unrelenting
Tiring
An existence based solely on survival.

The second man never wanted for anything
A self-confessed Mummy's boy,
An only child,
A brilliant student with scholarships and
funds from his
Parents and grandparents.
By twenty-four he had a Porsche
His parents were millionaires
But dodged the taxman.
Despite his affluence he still watched the
pennies

With a vigilant eye
He wasn't able to share, but he knew how
to accumulate
Designer clothes, shoes and multiple Apple
Macs
Whatever he had he always wanted more
Using his sharp mind to get it all
Until he grew fat with dollars and pounds
and euros.
And even when he had more than most, it
was still not enough
Because he wanted to realise his grand
ambition.
In order to do that
He needed oceans of cash, and it wasn't
about him
It was about fulfilling his vision
This vision of accumulation
What about altruism?
'Oh that will follow,' he would say glibly...
but only after he'd made at least
One billion.

The third man didn't care much for money
He was in love,
In love with his wife and children and the
dog
He lived for them
He thought only of them
Contemplating what he might buy for his
kids
The next holiday,
The second home,
The new car,
The perfume that his wife liked,

Dented

The books that his kids adored,
And even when his wife yelled and his
children got on his nerves
This man could only think of them.
His family defined his very essence
He gained strength from seeing them each
morning
He was dependent on them in every way
Their presence nourished his core
He was nothing without them.

The fourth man was alone in the world
Detached from family and friends
He was only interested in production
The production of words
The production of images
The flow of creativity was like a thousand
strong rivers
That kept his soul moist.
Without this production he felt brittle
On the verge of cracking.
His creativity was a gross vanity
Because, like the second man who
accumulated for himself,
The fourth man didn't care to share his
creativity with others.
He hoarded it all in a grand cupboard
And kept on producing
Like a baby excreting mindlessly.
The stuff just leaked out of the cavity
That was his unkempt mind:
'My duty is to make a mark each day until
the day I die,
To take my pen for a stroll in the universe,
like Paul Klee,

This is my reason for being.'

The fifth man
Worshipped the god of Dionysus
Woke up wanting
Craving for that fix
The rush of serotonin mixed with dopamine
And a dash of endorphins.
Whether he shot up,
Rolled a joint,
Slept with five thousand women,
Drove his cool car very fast,
Danced all night with a hard on,
His insatiable appetite for *fun,*
Kept him on the hunt,
Constantly looking over his shoulder
For something better:
Bigger tits
Longer legs
Plumper lips...
At twenty-five, thirty-five, forty-five, fifty-
five, sixty-five
His disposition didn't change.
He was an addict
In need of the 'greatest fuck of the
millennium'
That was beyond physical
He was seeking edification
The ultimate high
Wrenched from the febrile womb of
hedonism.

Survival
Accumulation
Dependence

Production
Edification

These are the five tenets of existence

Neither is more valid than the other,
Each man's life was marked by a specific
pointlessness
If she could be anything she would rather
be the -
Mindless producer,
The consistent shitter of shit
That sometimes resembled a lump of gold,
But only in her imagination.
It was still shit at the end of the day.
She pitied the first man who scraped for
rupees
She despised the avaricious waste of
accumulation
She thought love was a temporary,
unsustainable state
More often than not a disappointment and a
drain
She wondered if creative production was
simply a gross self-indulgence
Edification remained elusive because the
'ultimate' high didn't exist.
There would always be
More intense orgasms
And a deeper rush
To be tasted.

She slotted neatly into the fourth camp,
This was her rightful place
The spot where she belonged

And then she thought,
'If I could have the diligence of a sweat
shop worker,
The guilt free mind set of the accumulator,
The taste of love tattooed on my tongue,
The free flow of creativity,
The delirium that comes from intense
moments of pure pleasure
Surely then existence would be
meaningful?'

The perfect existence that encompasses all
five tenets
Who is living such an existence?
No one

Babies

I remember looking through the photo
album
Of my family
And counting two baby photos
If that
Perfect, I was
Honey skin, light reddish brown hair,
Button nose,
Tiny hands.

I remember sifting through albums a
second time
Thinking maybe there was a third or fourth
photo,
But there were none.
My mother said my late father used to take
the photos
He used to sing, too
Collect antiques and oil paintings
Drove a VW Beatle
When he died
Life stopped
Something died at the very core
Of this fragile family
Three years of nothingness
Three years without a single trace of my
being
Before someone picked up a camera again.

I remember thinking that I had no memory
Of day 0 to year 4 of my childhood
All I was told was that I cried
And cried and cried

Why did no memories come?
Was I burying something
Deep within
A place in my heart and mind
That I would rather forget?
Then I remember when my little sister was
born
And how day 0 to year 3 of her life was
clearly etched in my memory,
From the first moment when I examined
this perfect, brown bundle
With miniature hands and pillow soft skin.
She lay on a king sized bed,
Wriggling and squirming,
Gurgling and dribbling,
How I smiled when I looked at her.

I remember how joyless my mother was
She didn't realise the gift she'd been given
A fourth child at forty-three;
And when my little sister cried
I ran to her and wished that she would stay
small forever,
Just as I never wanted to grow up.
When my feet finally touched the ground as
I sat on the bus
No longer able to swing my legs,
Turning ten was the beginning of the end,
The end of watching the Mr Men and the
onset of the menstrual cycle and bee sting
breasts that began to swell.
The playground of childhood was beginning
to shrink
As the prison of adulthood inevitably closed
in.

I remember looking at photo albums of my
sisters' children
And how they documented every second,
Endless photos of endless joy.
They would make key rings
And mugs and calendars
Adorned with the faces of their spawn
As if trying to compensate for the absence
Of their own childhood memories.
Did that explain why I was so detached
now?
That I might not speak to a single member
of my family
For days
Weeks
Months
Years, even.

The birth of a child is a joy for most.
An old friend is about to have a baby
In a matter of weeks
'Are you excited?' I asked
'No,' he replied and hung his head low
'Do you fancy going clubbing tomorrow?' he
continued
Changing the subject
Almost trying to erase the fact that his life
Might change irrevocably
His coldness perturbed,
His ambivalence didn't surprise
I, too, was ambivalent about
Babies.

When the baby grows up

And loses the soft perfection that made
them so initially adorable
What happens when the promise and hope
Invested in this tiny bundle
Becomes lost?
What happens when all the proclamations that
'I will love my child no matter what'
Changes?

What happens if that precious gift
Becomes an obnoxious, spoilt little brat
And refuses to listen
Starts swearing aged three
Screams and yells
Gets spotty, lazy and fat
Fails their GCSES
Skives school
Flunks university
Goes on the dole
Becomes a teenage mum or dad
A drug dealer
Picks their nose and eats it
Never washes
Lives in filth
Has a sex change
Gets their body pierced and tattooed
Watches violent porn
Becomes a porno star
Is partial to heroin and coke
Addicted to sex
Develops kleptomania and pyromania
Gets arrested and does time for murder
Paedophilia
Torture and rape

Watches day time TV
Wets the bed
And flatulates in public

Would you still love your child?
Even if
All that promise turns to rot
All that hope turns to damned misery.

The idea of a baby makes me feel warm
The idea of creating something close to
perfection
Fills me with instant elation
The idea of cuddling and comforting a
helpless soul
Listening to a child's giggles and
Watching them sleep makes me almost cry,
But if my child wasn't perfect
Would I still love it?
Or reject it still?

Then I remember how I was the *perfect
child*
The model daughter
How I used to get up early
Make my pack lunch
Iron my uniform
Make the bed
Do the hoovering
Tidy up my mother's dressing table
Complete my homework without being
nagged
Strived for excellence without thinking
And still I was beaten and humiliated in
public,

But seldom ever cried
Was made to feel small inside
As a child and adult
The anger raged like a sea
That roars silently
Trapped in a hole
Waiting to burst forth
Building up since I grew in the womb.
Wouldn't want to make my child suffer
As I suffered
Wouldn't want to have a child
Simply to recreate
The childhood that I never had
Is that even possible?
Wouldn't want to deliberately 'fuck them up'
As Larkin said parents, subconsciously, do

If the baby would only stay a baby
And never grow up
If you could experience what it's like to
breastfeed
To play, to chase, to run with this
Curious bundle of wonder
Then I would have one tomorrow,
But they don't stay small forever
Babies always grow up in the end.

Dance On The Moon

A sad lonely girl stares at a small,
unobtrusive painting
That depicts the same forlorn, lonely girl
Standing in front of the mirror brushing her
teeth
She blinks mournfully.
When she opens her eyes
She sees a goddess in front of her,
Wearing burgundy lace satin underwear,
Seamed fishnets, suspenders and
Vertiginous heels.
She starts to hear the most
Sublime, delectable, delicious, euphoric
music
And begins to dance
Wildly and freely.
She takes flight and becomes a butterfly,
A bird, and then
A vivid creature
With an aquamarine, pink tipped tail.
She undresses until she is naked apart from
her red and gold heels
Adorned with lips
Still dancing, laughing and flying,
Then she sees an unobtrusive box of Lego
Lying all by itself in the middle of the floor.
In an instant
She starts to build a Lego spaceship with
nimble fingers
The spaceship smiles with gratitude and
takes off
Flying to Neptune
Holding her steady by the ankles

Landing softly
Where she rolls onto the vast crater filled
desert
And skips on the surface
Fingering herself gently and then violently
Until she comes
Puffing on a giant candy tasting spliff
That she lights up with a ray of sunshine.
She takes a deep drag and then
As she comes
She begins to scream so loud
The whole of the planet earth can hear her
Cry
That is a tender poem
A beam of mercury light
A silver stream of water
A tantalising breeze
A sear
A rush
A beast that devours the heart
And they all pause to listen and feel the
warmth of the golden orgasm
Penetrate the core of their being,
Like strawberries and cream laced with
chocolate,
And they sing in ecstasy -
The whole world, the stars and beyond.

Was

Was it wrong to shout back when someone
hurls turds at you?
Was it wrong to pick up the phone and try
to reach out?
Was it wrong to speak your mind?
Was it wrong to cry in front of a stranger?
Was it wrong to scream as you cycled
through London
Was it wrong to starve yourself because you
didn't think you were worth feeding?
Was it wrong to try to understand?
Was it wrong to sleep when everyone else
was awake?
Was it wrong to struggle and grapple for
hours on end?
Was it wrong to give up?
Was it wrong to say I don't know how to
make it work?
Was it wrong to close the door for good?
Was it wrong to not have the courage?
Was it wrong to have a vision?
Was it wrong to be the chosen one?
Was it wrong to be different from the
crowd?
Was it wrong that you were ever born?
Was it wrong that you did this instead of
that?
Was it wrong that you said nothing?
Was it wrong that you let someone make
you feel small?
Was it wrong when you couldn't say no?
Was it wrong when you couldn't say yes?
Was it wrong to walk away?

Was it wrong to spit instead of smile?
Was it wrong to continue?
Was it wrong to ever stop?
Was it wrong to give up on love?
Was it wrong to dismiss people?
Was it wrong to feel hate
Was it wrong to laugh when they were all
so serious?
Was it wrong to rush like a train?
Was it wrong to speak without breathing?
Was it wrong to feel something inside?
Was it wrong to see where the line would
take you?
Was it wrong to pause and linger?
Was it wrong to go back?
Was it wrong to want a fuck?
Was it wrong to puff on that joint and really
dig it?
Was it wrong to let someone you don't love
kiss you?
Was it wrong to go into a shop and steal a
paintbrush?
Was it wrong to want to come until your
pussy bleeds?
Was it wrong to refuse to sleep for days on
end?
Was it wrong to go through red lights with
your eyes closed?
Was it wrong to let strangers rape you
when manic and deranged?
Was it wrong to befriend your shadow?
Was it wrong to hide in a hovel?
Was it wrong to fight your corner?
Was it wrong to be a dreamer?
Was it wrong to want to be dead?

What is wrong?
And
What is right?
To
Speak in a mellifluous tongue
Look the fabulous part
Smile when you are supposed to
'How are you today?' someone randomly
asks
'Great,' you lie because to say
'I feel like utter shite,' just wouldn't do
Instead
We
Keep it all tucked in
Out of view
Because it's vulgar when a flabby gut hangs
out
For all the world to see

What is wrong and
What is right?

The only thing that you can try to be is
True

Yes

He nearly died
Stared death right in the face
Until then he'd been cruising
Maybe not caring
'I used to bash people up,' he said
And she tried to imagine him
Beating up the world.
'I don't love my mother,' he said with some finality,
His tone sinisterly sincere.
She tried to imagine him standing in front of his mother
Feeling nothing in his heart,
But she secretly didn't believe him.
'I left my girlfriend of seven years.
Once the door is shut it's over,'
He said with absolute finality.
She tried to imagine the moment his girlfriend walked into the hospital
Seeing him, the man she loved, lying there
He said, 'I knew and she knew,'
Without saying a single word
His love of seven years was finished.
Did it take his brush with death to understand what life means?
'I love life,' he said with a sparkle in his clear blue eyes
'Life is so beautiful.'
His mother was terrified of death, but fascinated at the same time
'Let's die together,' he said driving very fast
To the point when she cried, 'I don't want to die,' and wept

'OK so stop fucking saying you want to die,'
he snapped.
His tone was brutal and his mother
promptly shut up,
Even though her fears sat in the base of her
belly waiting to bite.
The skinny one saw his ruthless streak
clearly scored in his past
That side that could slice people up
Leaving them bleeding on the pavement.
What kind of woman was his mother, the
mother that he didn't love?
A woman who drove a doting husband far
away
A woman who set fire to her home
A woman who had never tasted love right
on the tongue
Or maybe she had and spat it out thinking it
was poison.
She was a vision to look at, all that beauty
What to do with it?
Was it a burden or a curse?
I envisage this woman
Old and worn like an antique teacup, sitting
by herself,
Indulging in morbid proclamations.
Occasionally, she recalls
A time when she held her infant son
He blinked at her with his ocean eyes
She whispered down to him, 'You are so
beautiful, you can conquer the world'
Hoping, too, that this little thing might give
her some strength
And love her 'til the day she died
Never realising that he would reject her

And dote on his father and brother instead.
'Just because you are biologically related
doesn't mean that you
will get on,' her sister once said.
Even though he tried to deny his love for his
mother
Sometimes he would look whimsical and
say,
'I like her more now she's become an old
lady'
This was his admission that she lived in a
small corner of his heart.
His eyes retained a glare of cyan coldness
That made them more alluring
Now he sat in his castle feeling happy
As his ship set sail across the world
And the skinny one thought of
How she had behaved in front of this man,
This man who said, 'You make me so
happy'
Thinking was she being real or wearing a
multitude of masks
Hiding what she really thought?
If he could see her now, melancholic,
defeated
Hiding away from the world without her
bright red lipstick,
No longer trying to be the person they all
wanted her to be,
Giving pleasure to strangers,
Laughing when her heart was squashed
tight,
Smiling when inside she was breaking,
Concealing her feelings for fear of ridicule,
But we must get on with it, mustn't we; it's

not an option to stop?
Someone always has an answer for
everything
What does that mean?
Does that mean that the skinny one was
beyond help?
Perhaps she was not the warrior she
aspired to be.

Now she rubs and rubs
Knowing the ink stain on the carpet is
permanent
She hand paints it
Hoping she can camouflage the unseemly
mark,
but it's always there
Forever
Now she hoovers knowing that the dust
mites will return with a vengeance
Now she listens to music knowing she will
get bored and seek other tunes
Now she paints knowing she is impatient to
paint the next one,
And the next.
As she struggles to keep her head held high
She feels she is sinking in a puddle of quick
sand
And still she tries to digest her plate of
curried turds with a smile.

Will she try to be like him?
Him
Who stared death right in the face,
Who has lumps on the insides of his
stomach to remind him of an *End* he

avoided with a sharp leap to the left
'I am broken too,' he says trying to reassure
her
Implying that they were not too dissimilar
But this made him even more remarkable
That he could still smile and
Sail the biggest ship on the fiercest seas.
She likes to paint herself as a wild beautiful
bird roaming free
Right then she inches forward like a
drugged up slug,
Wading through swathes of pus
That sticks and clings to everything.
It can be a lonely place to inhabit her world,
All the colour that was there
Only yesterday
Has been rubbed out with a giant eraser
She reaches out for her brush
Knowing that it will take her a lifetime to
repaint
All those dazzling colours
Then she sighs deeply
Her eyes start to overflow with hot tears
And she writes one word thinking of the
first thing he told her,
Which was simply
'Yes'.

Sad

I am sad
Very said
So sad
Sad now for too long
I know we have to put an end to this
sadness
No one understands our love
But us

As time passes
Was this love real?
Perhaps not
And if it was just a wild figment
Emanating from an overheated brain
I am sadder still

Think

I think of you
When I wake up
When I go to sleep
When I sit alone on a park bench and watch
strangers walk by
I think of you
And when you fall in love with another
I will still think of you

'Not likely that I will fall in love with anyone
else but you,' he replied

Years later, he does fall in love with another
Years later, she is long forgotten
Despised
Reviled
Denigrated
Years later, their doomed love seems like a
cruel joke
And a complete waste of time.

Dorothy

I met a lady called Dorothy
She was wearing aquamarine blue
I sat next to her on the plane
Dozed off thinking we had landed
Then I opened my eyes and said,
'Have we arrived?'
She laughed and said,
'We haven't even taken off yet.'
She was warm like a log fire
And we started to talk
About this and that
Small chat at first
Then family, relationships and children
'Ooh yes it's so expensive to bring them up'
'And the havoc they wreak on your body,'
she added
'The only advantage is your breasts get
really big...'
'But then they become smaller than they
were before,' she added wryly.
'I know women with deflated sacks with
downward drooping nipples, that's the price
of having a baby I'm afraid.'
'Wish you could blink and they would just
appear. How many do you have?' I asked
'Oh four, three girls and a boy'
'Wow what an achievement!' I exclaimed,
thinking what a nice granny she must be.
I pictured her as a retired old lady
With a doting husband and kids who cared
Just as she had all those years
And then she spoke in her ever so slight
Northern accent and it all came out,

Like a sudden spurt of water from a blocked
and swollen pipe.
'Unfortunately, I lost one daughter,' she
said forlornly
'My daughter worked in a man's world
And then she started to drink
And drink
And drink
We tried to help her
She was booked in at the Priory
Excited she was to go
And maybe glimpse Kate Moss.
She was in and out of hospital
Her legs bled water at one point
It all seeped out of her skin because her
Liver had collapsed.'
'Without the drink I have no reason to live,'
she said
She was pretty
Such lovely legs
And a slim figure
She had a boyfriend, but she got rid of him
Said he didn't understand
Went from job to job
Bed-sit to bed-sit
Ran up credit card bills
Ordered packages that remained unopened
We never gave up on her.'
Dorothy looked weary
Worn out like a battered carpet
That was once bright
With a thick bouncy pile.
'Then I got a call
The police found her dead,
All alone in her flat.

Dented

She said in a note that she had no one -
No family
That was hard to take
It tore the family apart.
We all grieve in our own way,
There are no big family gatherings,
The ones I had hoped for.
My son, he lives in Milan,
Doesn't get on with his sisters.
My daughter complains that I spend too
much time with my other grandson,
You can't please everyone.
My second daughter is trying for a child,
Four rounds of IVF,
Financially crippling,
Soul destroying it is.
She's thirty-eight now
So don't leave it too late will you?'
'What about your husband?
Doesn't he help?'
'Well we separated when the children were
young
I liked him, but he seemed to like other
women a lot more
Should have made a better choice really.'
I try to imagine Dorothy
This dignified, sweet and charming lady
Living on her own with her doting dogs
'Never had much of a career, was juggling
the children and trying to make ends meet
Now they're all grown up
But they don't get on like I wish they did...'
She doesn't grumble or complain
Just reflects in her soft and quiet voice.
I don't tell her how I seldom speak to my

mother
But I do say that happiness comes in small
stabs
Since you never know when you are going
to get your next dose,
Better to relish the few seconds of
sweetness that come your way.
I watch as she embraces her old friend
who's been waiting for her.
Another grey haired old lady.
Wish her a happy holiday
Long sleepy, sunny days
Time to forget that sharp pain
That jabs at her heart
With a serrated edge;
And I think of Marian her daughter
With her lovely legs as Dorothy described
them.
She was thirty-five when she died
My age
Same age as my late father
I wonder if they have collided up there in
heaven
Marian and my Daddy
Are they watching us?
Saying, 'It's ok, enjoy your life'.
Marian's having a drink and my Daddy's
singing
They are both squatting on clouds
Smiling and laughing.

Agata

When you said, 'I think perhaps you do not
trust me'
You were right
In many ways
But how am I supposed to trust someone
Who has never addressed me by name?
Nor greets with a smile?
And finishes when those fifty minutes are
up - unless you are late?
You are not culpable
In fact you are exercising a professional
detachment
This is how you were trained
Understand that it is nothing personal,
But then how do you expect me to walk into
that dull box
That is the therapy room
And pour my guts out
Cry in front of you
Spread my soul on those walls
As you sit with a face like stone and speak
with a voice that is
Disingenuously gentle.
I've seen how you look at my attire, my
bare legs
And I wonder,
'Is she judging me like all the rest?'
Well you once said, 'You do dress sexily?'
Do I?
So should I dress like you then?
And when I look at your face
An implacable expression is all I see.
Try to think beyond the mask

Your life in Poland, your past and present
life
Try to see the world through Agata's eyes
Maybe some days you don't feel like waking
up?
Maybe you don't want to face your clients?
Maybe you switch off as we whine and cry
and moan?
Maybe you think of your own woes?
Maybe some days you don't care?
But you wear that polished mask
You remember the details that we spew and
fire them out
Like soft missiles
And watch as they swiftly penetrate and our
lower lips tremble like clockwork:

We break a little more

As you try to map out a picture of an
already broken soul.
You say that I am a starving orphan who
never received the love and affection that I
craved
You say I didn't get enough of my mother's
milk
You say that I am sucking on that stale
grain of rice that
Represents my relationships,
But you don't say how to get out of the
dump
You don't tell me how to change the tape
and listen to a new song
You cannot give me the panacea that I
dream about,

Because there is no panacea.
The only thing that we can be sure of is
getting old, sick and
Dying alone
And what of your pain Agata?
Do you tuck it away neatly from public
view?
Do you bare your soul to a stranger?
Do you have a husband?
Children
A dog
A home
A garden
A good life?
The good life that we all want
At least we think we want.
And then I think of Dr Morgan my
psychotherapist
Dr Bass my psychiatrist
And I think of the mess that is probably
their minds,
Which they are still trying to unravel
Like a tightly knotted, colossal ball of string,
Which they hide in a drawer in their office
As they grapple with the mess that is other
people's lives.
And we are all entangled in this big ball of
string
That has become matted and mangy
Congealed and yellow.
So when you ask me, 'I think perhaps you
do not trust me'
It is true
But then how can I trust anyone?
When the very people that were closest

Shattered the walls I constructed as a child
to protect me.
When I think of the many hundreds I have
collided with
The friends that have all but gone
The stones that tried to break this bony
frame
The strangers that wedged in their feeble
rods at will and then
Discarded what was left like trash
The husband who abandoned his wife
The men who make lewd remarks on the
street
The women who smile and bite at the same
time
The men that hurl abuse like arrows
The rich and famous that come preying and
then promptly flee
And even when someone pays me a
compliment
That smells of honey
Or someone says, 'You are wonderful'
I am incapable of digesting this delicious
food
And decline their offerings of praise and
adulation
Preferring the familiar sound of invective
bile
And the sting of a rebarbative tongue
That is the only milk I know how to guzzle
without puking.
So, Agata,
Oh sage one,
And I say this without a shred of sarcasm
You tell me

Dented

How is it possible for me to ever trust
anyone at all
Let alone you?

Spent

'I am so tired,' she whispered
Staring into the two wells of darkness that
were pushing deeper into her skull
'Spent'
Where have all the people gone?
The mother who brought her into this world
A shrinking dumpling that seemed frail now,
Absent and forgetful,
A stepfather with no teeth and a seemingly
innocuous soul,
Riddled with secrets buried and hidden,
Siblings that were strangers,
People whom she loved as if her life
depended on it,
Fair weather friends whom she never
turned to,
For fear that they might see her weakness -
Where were they all now?
'Must be strong,' she whispered
Invincible like god.
Her nipples poked out of the rainbow dress
That dazzled London
As she flew down the streets
With no petrol in the tank.
'I am burnt out'
Beauty fading by the day,
Slashed wrists,
Neatly carved like beautiful glass sculptures,
Body arranged in an elegant pile of bones,
On a bed of blood,
Her soul dancing in pools of black,
Darting between the clouds,
Soaring with other spent souls,

Making silent love,
Interweaving and rubbing against invisible
particles.
'What now?' she didn't know
There was nowhere left to run
They all saw her scars
Thousands of them knitted together
To make a sheet of diaphanous fractured
skin
Veins pumping green,
Like the rivers of Bangladesh.
'When will I return?'
She didn't know
Would the lips of a hungry child ever suckle
her breasts?
Would that miracle grow in her belly?
These questions she crumpled,
Cut up and
Scattered the shreds.
'Shining light' that's what you were
'Dwindling light' that's what she was
Thirty-five
A sacred number
A perfect age
Neither old nor young
An ideal moment
To take a leap
Not knowing what was down below
'What lies behind those eyes?'
'Who is the woman who remains a girl?'
Too tired to unpick these questions
Spent

The French Boy

She'd known him now for a year or more
A year of random collisions
And fleeting conversations
Encounters dripping with a subtle French
charm
And sly coquettish ways.
She was shy around him
Always happy to see his charming face
He saw her come and go
She looked out for him
Sometimes he would appear out of the
shadows
Come up behind her
And suddenly spoke in his French accent
Gently startling, unleashing something
warm inside.
When she learnt of his age, a mere 'twenty
six'
She thought, *he is but a boy*
Was never sure if he liked her that way
'Perhaps he thinks of me as a granny?'
When she finally disclosed her age
It didn't seem to matter as he asked
'What would you like darling?'
And then he disappeared
Before serving her fresh mint tea
His heart was still wounded from a past love
affair
With a girl he thought he might marry and
have children with one day.
Women came up to him
Propositioned him for illicit liaisons,
But he always refused

Although perhaps once or twice he gave in -
Well, he was human and French.
He saw her drawing on a rooftop
He watched her film on the BBC
He googled her
And began to understand that this 'granny'
was armed with a
Mighty talent
That she hid in her fingertips and chocolate
brown eyes
He went to her exhibition
Even though he was tired and drained,
Spent solitary minutes staring into her
world.
He saw her with various men
And sometimes wondered about her private
life
Were they lovers or friends?
She never gave anything away,
But always greeted him with a smile and
amiable, delightful chat.
Then one day he texted her and she replied
What made him choose that moment?
'I am very shy, I need to get drunk to find
the courage,' he confessed
They almost missed one another
Then she found him fumbling in the dark
They got stoned
Talked about everything and nothing
He played his reggae music
And then he said with a slight
awkwardness, 'Can I give you a massage?'
She didn't know whether to oblige him
In the end she succumbed
And then they kissed and had sex

His eyes were closed most of the time,
Was he thinking about the big love of his
life?
She didn't mind
She learnt long ago that when you yearn
you suffer.
This was another moment
In a long line of moments
One that she would remember
He caressed her through the night,
He kissed her gently,
And he smelt like a flower,
Even in the morning
When they parted.
She knew that they would collide again
He would smile and say, 'Bonjour
mademoiselle'
And she would beam back and kiss him
gently on the cheeks
Steal a glance as he rushed around
Serving demanding customers
Always with beguiling charm and
conversation.
This French boy loved his wine
Fine cuisine and warm company
He grew up with artists in the French
countryside
And now he was finding his way in the city
Dreaming of his restaurant
That one day he could call his own.
Perhaps he would hang one of her paintings
on the walls
Let her doodle in the toilets
Or doodle on his skin.
These words are about a French boy

Dented

A tender, simple creature
With pale skin and ocean blue eyes
That shone a little brighter when he saw
her.

What's The Difference?

What's the difference between
The lover whom you fuck
And a man whom you love?
To be fair sometimes you make love to the lover
Or should I say fuck gently and tenderly
Where lies the difference, you might ask?
The difference lies in the nuances that we often overlook
We seldom find the lover that interesting
Mentally it's almost impossible to engage
With him
Since what intrigued us in the first place
Was rather superficial
Such as a large appendage
A splendid physique
A pretty boy face
Something very nice to look at
When they open their mouths'
They usually talk about
Their petty selves; they are not engaged
With the world
Not one bit
Even when you are talking
They are never really listening
Because you are the fleapit that they prod,
Lick and stick
Something into.
Don't much like being fucked particularly
Lovers are not quite present
Seldom are they right there in the moment
They much prefer to gaze at their cock as it slides in and out

Dented

Like a coy snake
Or they like it from behind
Ramming it in and out
In and out
An incessant motion
That makes them feel like
The king of the world.
You soon realise that you are a piece of
tender meat with legs
You just want him to come so that
It can be over and then you can sleep,
Because you've come three times already
And what else is there to do?
You are getting sweaty
Make up all smudged
Love making or fucking,
Is fast losing its allure.
Lovers sound good on paper
They are fun to boast about,
A bore in reality
Once the climax has been reached
It's: 'Thank you very much,' and time to
Get the hell away from them
Reading Tagore is more stimulating
Painting more profound
Cycling more exhilarating.
Lovers leave their residue
Their clumsy mess
Sex stains and stink
They seldom have any finesse
Worse than this is a lover who wants you to
stay over
And pretends that he cares
When all he wants is to get a suck and
second shag in the morning,

Before he predictably kicks you out so that
he can start his day
Politely of course
Gladly for sure
Or with a curt slam of the door.
And if you fall in love with a lover
Then you are fucked
And deserve every sorry scenario that
comes your way:
Cold indifference
Perpetual belittlement
Sustained dissatisfaction
Prolonged silence.
A life that consists of a steady string of
lovers
Is a life of transient highs and chronic
Cavernous
Bewildering
Emptiness.

Now the man whom you love
The one who has remained a constant hum
Whatever metaphorical brick you have slung
at him
Is the man who has seen you bare faced
and still finds you beautiful
Or physically tolerable at least
The one who listens even when you are
boring the shit out of him
The one who lets you cry like a baby until
Snot trickles and your body is shaking.
The man whom you love is the one
You can reveal everything to,
Scoop out your soul
And throw it in his face

Especially the strange idiosyncrasies
Exposing the bits that make others run a
fucking mile
He gets you
He digs you
He wants to be with you
He's dreamt about growing old with you
He's envisaged the kids that are yet to be
born
He wants to take care of you
Without obligation,
But happily with a smile.
There is no mask
No pretense
No modification or gentle tiptoeing
When he says he will call
He calls
And if you are moody he will ask why first
If you shout he might shout back,
But you know that it will always blow over
End up in a firm hug
Or safe coexistence.
The man whom you love
Is the one you eat breakfast, lunch and
dinner with
The first person you see when you wake up
The last person you see when you close
your eyes
He won't blank you even when you have
been a bitch
He remembers the purple period
Although the relationship has gone brown
Around the edges
And sometimes you become two remote
islands

Circling one another
Not quite letting go
Sometimes you don't talk and ignore one
another for years,
But never walk out the door.
The man whom you love is loyal, not fickle
Or vicious like the wind
He might lapse,
Because we all do
He might fall in love with another
Yet no woman will ever surpass you
He will always love you more
And you know it
As you stick firmly in the back of his mind
Like a hardened piece of chewing gum
Wherever he is
Whatever he's doing
Even when he's traveling to the other side
of the world
Even when he's coming inside younger flesh
Even when he's having a good time with his
mates
Even when he's lost in his work
When he closes his eyes
He sees only you staring back at him
You are always there
Wherever

Because he loves you

Here lies the difference between a lover
whom you
Fuck
And a man whom you
Love

Bits of Luck or Perilous Misfortune

N. S. Naipaul spoke with methodical
conviction about
The bits of luck that punctuated his life
The bits of luck that made him the great,
Esteemed Nobel Prize winning writer of
today
And as she listened
Seduced by the cadence of his weathered
voice
She began to think
About the bits of luck that she had once
deemed as perilous misfortune.
The luck to be dismissed as stupid, which
allowed her to shine surreptitiously
The luck to be abused, which helped her to
understand what it was to be loved
The luck to know from the age of four that
she wanted to be an artist
The luck to never let that dream die when
many tried to trample upon it
The luck to ride a wave of flowing
uninterrupted creativity
The luck to get into Oxford University
The luck to lose her coveted place knowing
that to go would have meant a sudden
death
The luck to be sexually assaulted, which
allowed her to see the nasty toxic mud
under the glossy shine of hope
The luck to discover a love of art that would
remain unrivalled in her lifetime

The luck to discover a whole new world of
shiny innocence when her little sister was
born
The luck to go to the LSE where she met
the first big love of her life, a man who led
her down a different path
The luck to get into Chelsea School of Art
and Design
The luck to discover that Art College would
destroy her, so better to drop out
The luck to discover finally what it was to
write, to watch the layers of meaning
become richer as she plucked sentences
from the air
The luck to be awarded a scholarship to film
school where she honed a new craft
The luck to fail abysmally before she could
ever really learn
The luck to start painting again with a
voracious passion at twenty-three
The luck to land a solo show without even
trying
The luck to find allies when she thought she
had none
The luck to model, travel the world, publish
books and meet great minds and lesser
ones, too
The luck to still have beauty that stubbornly
refuses to fade
The luck to find a lover who taught her
what it was to taste passion
The luck to have many more lovers who
made her realise the value of one love
The luck to be abandoned in order to
discover it was ok to be alone

The luck to want to die only to realise that
she actually wanted to live
The luck to build a humble home with her
very own hands
The luck to be diagnosed as *mad* and find
method in her madness
The luck to turn alchemy into gold
The luck to be alive today when her father
died at the same age
The luck to still be scribbling with a pen in
her hand and a paintbrush clenched
between white teeth
The luck to learn
To play like a child,
Dance like a fiend
And make music in lush parallel worlds
The luck to refuse to enter the concrete box
where adults loitered
The luck that could have easily been
perilous misfortune
The bits of luck that make up life
That we string together like precious pearls
That gleam around our necks.

Everyone has bits of luck
If only we try not to forget

The Colours

The sound of revelry drifted through
A hot summer evening
People laughed, drank and ate
Content to be with one another
For hours and hours
A modern definition of a good time
She was tempted to go out and
Get stabbed by the knife of hedonism
Wielded by attractive strangers,
But stayed put instead.
Wrapped up tight in a cloak of solitude
Holding onto a paintbrush for dear life
Watching as the strokes breathed
And weaved slowly and deliberately
One by one.
The colors
Began a complex conversation
That was difficult to follow,
A different sound,
A silent dialogue
That tingled and sang
And made no sense
At all
The harsh sound of revelry
Distracted her by the second
The sound of snorting pigs
Made her want to scream
Each tried to compete
To impose
Dominate
Subjugate
As the paintbrush battled
The colors roared delicately

Ridiculous hoots of laughter made her
cringe
And pull a foul grimace
As they continued to deride
The paintbrush grew weary
Trapped in a viscous mess
In time those nasty poking sounds abated
And the colors were victorious in the end
Dancing and making love in the wind.

Settle

Cold indifference
Stingy, foul kisses
An abrupt push
Blank eyes
She realised
Tonight
That he didn't love her anymore
That it was, unequivocally, over
That it had been for a long time.
She slipped her wedding ring back on a
bony finger
Was reborn a virgin
And would walk away
Close the door
Try to forget
Try to move on
Try to push him out of her head
She hoped never to see him again
She hoped that if she did she would feel
nothing
She hoped that he would fade away.
The nights were long
The music was not enough
The art was not enough
There was a hunger in her belly
That might never be fed
But better to go hungry
Than settle for a measly kind of love
A love that leaves you broken
Weak and small
Better to settle for a token ring on her
finger instead.

Roast Chicken and Potatoes

I know four men
These four men I regard as my friends
They see me as a curious, lithe, clever little
creature
The one thing that unites them is a
  a) Seasoned brand of intelligence, rare
     to find
  b) Economic solvency, comes in handy
     in this material world
  c) And a charming, generous manner -
     even rarer still
In short they are the epitome of *success*
And doesn't everyone want to be
successful?
I define all four of them as:
A delectable plate of roast chicken and
potatoes
They all seem to covet the description
These men value my opinion about women
They know that I will be honest
That I have no
Ulterior motive to be mendacious
That I prefer carrots to potatoes
So I say to them,
'Listen, when women see you they want to
devour the sustaining meal that you are,
but you must choose the guests that sit at
your table very carefully,
The next decision that you make will be
critical,
The one who consumes you must relish
every bite,
Not regurgitate or spit you out.

And remember once you have been
Eaten and digested
That's it.'
The four men listened carefully and nodded
in agreement urging me to continue,
'Don't be blinded by a woman's beauty,
The alluring fleshiness of her breasts,
The elegance of her slender ankles and
toes,
The dreamy profundity you think you see in
her eyes,
Beauty makes women invisible.
Peel back the layers and take a good
Long hard look at her soul,
You will see mouldy rankness and the dense
Wonder of unexplored thorny forests,
There will be gloomy caves and vast
swathes of light;
It will take time to upturn every rock and
explore each crevice
That makes up the painting of her soul.'
'But I am carnal,' number one interjected
'I need to feel like a virile man, there's a
time to fuck you know,' number two
continued
'I want to see if she is domesticated,'
number three said somberly
I replied, 'Yes we are animals and
sometimes we need to eat
And yes we live in a time when men are
emasculated.
They feel redundant like flaccid cocks
As for being domesticated get a maid to
iron your underpants before you let
someone sully your palace.

Remember it's easy to start a relationship,
But not that easy to end it.
Life is a line that we draw with our own
hand
Be careful what kind of relationship you
scribble
Once scribbled, extrication is seldom easy.'
Number two then said philosophically,
'Sometimes it is better to have nothing than
everything'
'If you deny yourself the 'want'
You will liberate your soul', I added.
'Yeah but you are living your life as a
celibate monk,' number four said scornfully
'This is not about me, it's about the four of
you
The choices that you make
Might help to construct a new prison that
incarcerates you for another ten years or
sets you free.'
'But the problem is they want to get
married and have children,
I've done that, been there,' number 2 piped
'Me too,' added number 4
'I want a family, the time is right for me,'
said number 1
'I had a kid at 27 and now I have a new
son, 27 years later, with a girl I am
ambivalent about,' number 4 said
mournfully.
'I am bored, I want to have an affair,' he
said with a hint of petulance.
'None of you realise that you can have
whatever you want

Right now imagine that you are standing in
a sweet shop,
You have an array of delicious sweets laid
out before you,
Hand picked and arranged, but of course it
is not possible or feasible to consume all of
them simultaneously:
Bon Bons, toffee chews, cola fizzes and
sherbet dips
Consumed all together they will make you
puke,
But individually for sure they're an absolute
delight.
Simply
Think before you chew and suck,
Scrutinise each and every one because
outwardly they may appear sweet,
But once bitten they could break all your
teeth or lead to decay...
If I am honest when I think about the men
in my life
If I think long and hard,
What did they bring me?
Not fucking much
Just a lot of hassle
Don't wear that
Don't say that
Don't do this
Or dare do that
They criticised my personality
Or parts of my body,
Called when they felt like it
Ignored when they felt like it, too.
They tried to lock me in a gilded cage or a
tiny shack,

But I always escaped like the exotic bird of
paradise that I am.
What will these women bring to you?
Apart from their obvious beauty
Their sinewy legs
Their firm bodies
Their dreamy eyes
Their glossy locks and a neatly shaven
pussy.
'It's all about pussy,' number 2 piped
'So that's what it boils down to – pussy?'
'Absolutely,' number 2 cried
'I wonder if men really want an intelligent
woman?
Surely you want a subordinate, beautiful
creature that...
Is intelligent, but not
Too intelligent?
And they should worship their man,
See him as a demi-god,
Be a mother, a lover, a maid and a scholar.'
'Yes,' they all cried
'That's exactly what we want'
'Maybe she does exist out there,
You just might not live to ever meet her
Until then lick slowly
And masticate tentatively
Enjoy the now
Forget the past
One day we will all be dead.'

The Famous

What makes the famous
Famous?
The fact that a select few
Have colossal mammaries
Exquisite erudition
Intoxicating beauty
Mind blowing talent
A distinct pedigree
What makes them so special
To distinguish them from
The rest?
And why do people want so desperately to
be famous?
As if fame is the ultimate prize.
I met Jude Law, the actor, in the lift,
On a rainy afternoon in London.
Was wearing a big hat
With my head lowered
Then he stood right in front of me
Looked up
Was startled to see him.
One year ago, when I was in New York,
He called me
Proposed rather curtly that we should meet
Then he never called back.
And so I looked him in the eye,
In that very cramped lift,
After he smiled disingenuously, and I asked
'What happened in New York?'
'I fell asleep and then I lost my phone in
Cuba and your number, too'
So that makes it alright does it? I whispered
silently.

I noticed as he spoke the slight whiff of
halitosis -
With all his millions why he didn't
Make a swift trip to the dentist
Or even buy some dental floss?
I watched as he chatted up the receptionist
An easy lay perhaps
Would she be chucked in the bin
Like a chocolate wrapper
Or a piece of soiled bog roll?
He bought me a drink
Was perplexed that I requested a Virgin
Mary
Raised his finger to remove some fluff
Stuck to my jaw
Trembled as he touched me
Felt increasingly awkward
Out of place
Afraid of saying the wrong thing
So whipped out my sketch book,
Which left him more baffled
Probably wasn't his sort of girl
Although something attracted him to me
What exactly?
You have to ask the A list movie star
Maybe it was just sport?
Reeling women in
Only to toss them back in the sea
After snaring them with his rusty twisted
hook.
Told me casually to come to a party
Then walked away
Leaving me lagging behind
As if I really didn't count
It was at this party that

I met another *famous* person
Mr Stephen Fry
One with more intellect by far
Our brains had more in common maybe
He was polite and charming
And resembled a noble, weathered tree
Told him how I had grown up with his face
on the screen
Admired his use of long words
How the juxtaposition of *cunt* and
mellifluous
Made the English language rich and juicy
Told him how I enjoyed his documentary
about manic depression
And thought it was brave
Told him, too, that being mentally ill was a
curse and a blessing
A gift and a hindrance
How it could make us soar and render us
Half dead and glued to the bed for days.
As I spoke I began to withdraw thinking
I am not worthy to speak to these people,
Just a tiny particle
Floating uselessly in the universe,
And skulked away
(Even though I was the best dressed by far
At that sad excuse for a party).
Found a hole
On Bethnal Green Road
And crawled right in
Where no one could find me
Plucked out a magic pen
And felt sane again
As I drew furiously
Methodically and

Beautifully.

So you are in a mediocre over hyped film
That makes you famous
So you write a second-rate hyped book
That makes you famous
So you have ginormous tits
That makes you famous
I spit on fame and the division it brings
Fame is for losers.

Spot

Spot on her bottom
Spot on her thigh
Spot on her forehead
Spot on her belly
'Don't worry these ugly spots will go away'
'But why do they come in the first place?'
'The one on your bottom arrived in protest
because you have been eating too much
chocolate cake
The one on your forehead poked through
because of lack of sleep
The one on your thigh is not a spot,
A mosquito bit you
She flew all the way from Bangladesh to
avenge the death of
Her brother you squashed with your thumb
And the one on your belly isn't a spot either
Just a blemish that refused to disappear for
two years,
Frankly, you couldn't tolerate the
imperfection
Dared to think you could scratch it away
Cut it out with a knife
Admired your clumsy handiwork
Before realising it looked ten times worse.
If you'd left it alone no one would have
known
In fact most of the marks on your body
Were self-inflicted in the quest for
Perfection.
Forget these spots
They are superficial anyway

Dented

Irrelevant
Minor imperfections
Forget how you look
Who cares?
Everyone has spots, marks, scars
Some discoloration on the skin
Or suppurating wound
That won't ever heal
They are vital to our existence.
The world is made up of dots and circles
and tiny little spots,
Making an even bigger, giant dot
That is the universe.

The Jewish Man and the Pen

She was immersed in words
Music was blasting her eardrums into
deafness
A tall, corpulent Jewish man boarded the
train
Wearing traditional dress
With long curly locks dangling freely against
each cheek,
He removed his shoes and positioned them
on the seat in front,
A white toe wriggled through the hole in his
sock
And the sharp, pungent stink of unwashed
feet wafted her way
He made a call and began to talk in his
native tongue
Loudly with a constant nasal
'Aaaa-uuuh'
It was an offensive noise
A substitute for 'excuse me'
However loud she turned her music up she
couldn't
Obliterate those rude interruptions
She felt him trying to get her attention
Knew that he was eyeing up her pen
A Staedtler pen with a 0.05 nib
A pen she bought in New York
A pen she used to draw her epic panoramic
sky scapes
And she ignored him,
Deliberately.
She wasn't going to lend him his pen
Because of his obtrusive big toe

His offensive noises
And his obstreperous chatter,
Yet she had at least one hundred pens
In her bag
How uncharitable of her not to lend this
man a pen.
In the end he got her attention and asked
politely
'May I borrow a pen?'
'No, I'm sorry sir these are my drawing
pens'
It was a lie; it was possible to write with
them, too.
She felt ashamed momentarily
What was he thinking?
'Aaagh anti-Semitism is rife,
This girl does not lend me a pen
When she has a thousand,
You see the whole world is against us
You see, you see...
We have to fight for a pen
It has come to this
What a sad world we live in'.
And she silently replied,
'It has nothing to do with you being Jewish,
It has to do with you
And your big toe wiggling at me
Your stinky feet
Your selfish telephone manner and
Your total disregard for others on this train
You tell me one good reason why I should
lend you this pen?'
Was this how racism became rampant?
Was this how people felt vilified, snubbed
and marginalised?

Did it all stem from the refusal to lend a pen
to a stranger?
She'd never know because
They never did have
A frank and honest discussion;
She never complained about the smell, the
toe, or the noise
And he never quizzed her as to why she
refused to lend him
A pen when she stashed scores in her bag.
The answer to these questions remained
Unanswered, twisted and manipulated into
Another kind of dubious,
Alternative truth
That all stemmed from a humble
Pen

Scribbles and Bullets

'I do feel sad about the way people treat
each other, but it's impossible to shift
stones that have grown roots
And even though there is love
These roots run deep'.
These words did not comfort the skinny one
and in reply she said to her little sister
'Stones that have grown roots
No one is asking you to shift them
It is not your role to do so
And these are not stones
These are a flurry of bullets that come firing
at any time, in any direction'.
The skinny one did not have a single finger
on the trigger
She came home with reservations,
Still she came peacefully
With zero expectations and yet...
The bullets come fast
She tried to duck, but each time they hit
They lodged deep in the flesh
Leaving her bleeding,
A trickle at first and then the blood vomits
from the mouth of the wound,
Standing in a small ocean of blood
Was she supposed to turn the other cheek?
Snide taunts,
Cheap bullying
Irrational outbursts
Unpredictable tempers
And finally
Public humiliation for all to see
Was she supposed to stay quiet as she once

did?
Relive a childhood that she would rather
just forget?
How she has tried to make amends
Rationalise
Make excuses
Since she was a small child
And as she has grown into the slender,
sensitive adult that she is today
She grows ever smaller
Ever diminishing
'When I go home I become a baby without
nappies
Crawling on all fours,' she said.
The skinny one recalled how she tried to
protect her younger sister
From the madness and violence that she
was born into
How different it would have been if she'd
simply ignored her
Now this same little sister is trying to 'shift
the stones that have grown roots'
An elegant metaphor she believed perfectly
described the situation
That was the 'family'
Her little sister meant well, she was a wise
soul in a young teenager's body
She wanted to rearrange
The stones in a pattern that
Was beautiful.

'There is a reason why I stay away.
You will never understand what it feels like
to suffer alienation within your own home.
I came to meet my niece, I have met her

now.'
The skinny one had completed her sisterly
duty
The moment she saw that perfect face, the
pure smile and dimpled cheeks
She felt a joy and it reminded her of the
elation
When she held her little sister
When she held her first nephew
Now that first nephew was a spotty
teenager
Who smoked roll ups at fourteen
He carried the weight of glumness on his
shoulders
The skinny one knew he understood
The torment she endured
At the hands of his erratic thoroughly
damaged mother,
Her funny ways, her vicious tongue that
could suddenly become...
Sweet and forgiving.
He also ducked and dived to avoid the
bullets that came firing
Out of the angry gob of his mother
The skinny one remembered his innocence
as a child
His charm and beauty, his infectious
laughter -
He was sullen now
Trapped in an interior world
That had walls and no *small tent of blue*.
He stood over the skinny one as she drew
Made her breakfast in an attempt to get
closer, but there was an
Innate awkwardness between them

As if they both knew the bond they could
have forged
Would never be.
The closeness she wanted to cultivate
remained
An imagined one in her head
The same would happen with her new
niece,
There was only a glimmer of a connection
with her second nephew.
The skinny one could only stare in
wonderment at his
Piercing blue, green eyes
Observe his naughty ways and cherish this
As a rare memory.

Packing her bags the skinny one walked out
Thinking of the words that were said,
'Your gaunt face is scaring the baby, make
your eyes smaller then she will stop crying,'
yelled her middle sister
'Don't photograph the baby, ask permission
first, she's my daughter,' her big sister
cawed
'Don't force him to eat, don't crowd him'
'Don't give them those toys to play with'
'I can talk to you the way I like and if you
don't like it go'
'Why can't you wear longer skirts?'
'Why don't you wear flat shoes?' my middle
sister continued.

Why don't you just jump off the highest cliff
and die?

Dented

She knew no one would come running,
She knew that everyone was glad when she
skulked away
She knew that no apology would be
forthcoming
There was a family
But she was not part of it,
She couldn't relate to any single member
The skinny one was an alien
And the only way she could process the
pain was by transforming it
Into a feeble kind of art.

What do you do when 'home' is not the safe
nest?
You hoped it to be
What do you do when
Home has become a suffocating shed?
A bloody war zone
Do you leap from the bridge that you have
drawn with your own hand?
To escape those flying poisoned daggers
Or do you keep on scratching, trying to
unearth elusive meaning?

'As I slide down the curve of a hill that my
hand tries to conjure
I see dried up rivers that start to bleed
Into my soul,
And yet
The hand that
Doodles is never still.'

The skinny one began to disconnect from
this nebulous concept called
Home
Home was making her ill
Home had become her sickness
Home equalled *Hell*

Before when she looked at the painting that
she called 'family'
She saw her place in the composition
Now the painting was a brown smudge of
canine excrement
It was futile trying to make a house out of
water
It was better to swim on down the stream
And hedge your bets in the middle of the
sea
Even if you might drown.

Caged Animal

He was pitiful and diminutive
Lying in a walk way with open sores on his
Emaciated, haggard excuse of a face.
He didn't care if people kicked or spat at
him
No one saw the cage that was his cell
The invisible bars that he peered out of
He became a caged animal
Pacing up and down,
Back and forth,
Scratching for a way out,
But no way out came.
Once upon a time he was a baby
Covered in blood and then washed clean
Close to perfect for a few seconds, days,
months and years
When did his skin become so pitted?
Memories of his parents were a blurred
Dense white haze.
Once upon a time he had ambition
'If you work hard you will be rewarded
If you try in the end you will succeed'
That's what they dished out at school
That's what he lapped up and digested
That's what he believed.
The consecutive failures that dogged each
Year of his existence left him apathetic
It was easier to call himself a 'stinking loser'
It was easier to lie in his cage and still get
his head kicked in
He saw beautiful couples kissing as they
parted goodbye
Pregnant women with expanding waistlines

And growing broods
He saw old wrinkly Bengali men with
multiple wives,
One, two and three
He saw groups of friends
Units
Clusters
Tribes
Gangs
He saw loners too, but they wore polished
masks
That left them protected
He saw how others seemed to crack the nut
That only broke his teeth when he bit on it
He once tasted the sweet honey of love on
his tongue
Touched skin that left him soaring
Came more times than he could count,
But the woman he loved flew away when
she saw this man
She was not strong, but frail and timid
He always thought she would leave in the
end
And when she did, his self-imposed isolation
Began to strangle him slowly
He paced up and down his cage
Knowing that he could walk out if he
wanted to
Incarceration was the distant relation of
Liberation.
For years now he sat in that stinking hovel
he dug for himself
'You are your own worst enemy,' his
estranged brother yelled.
Did he drive them all away?'

Dented

The cage grew smaller by the day
And he grew smaller still in the cage
Losing all hope that he would ever escape
this self created hell
People drink water to quench their thirst
He yearned to drink bleach to burn out his
heart
People wake up eager to start their day
He preferred to sleep for an eternity
People dream
He lay awake, drenched in blood
People laugh
Inside he wept
People stare
He looked away
People make love
He lay alone and occasionally wanked
People eat
He slowly wasted away, refusing all food.
Who was this homeless man?
Lying in a flea-ridden sleeping bag of
Sweat and shit
Who was he?
This homeless man
Was me

The Smelly Old Man

She had never heard of the artist
Cy Twombly
Everyone said that the exhibition at the
Tate was 'arresting'
Whatever she might think
It was surely interesting to see an artist's
work
From start to finish in one lifetime
To scrutinise a corner of an artist's vision
To begin to comprehend what one vision
can possibly consist of.
The white canvases and carved out marks
were curious,
The splashes of colour, the drips, the swirls,
the vastness of it all -
Intriguing.
There were sculptures of found objects
welded together,
Left outside in rainstorms to rust and be
reborn
A fragile rose coated in white paint,
Suspended and nailed to a block of gnarled
wood
She entered one room that was surprisingly
empty and then she saw him
A squat hunch of a man with white greasy
hair
Pulled into a messy ponytail.
There was a sweat mark on his back that
looked like the outline of an African
continent,
And he exuded the reek of flesh that hadn't
been washed in a decade.

His cheeks looked like they had only been
kissed twice out of begrudging pity,
His shoes were perhaps once worn by
Charlie Chaplin,
His hound dog eyes lapped up the art,
He inched as close as he could until his
bulbous nose almost touched the paintings;
Then he caught the skinny one staring at
him.
Their eyes interlocked in a gaze that was
prolonged
By a second too long
The skinny one was alone, just like that
smelly old man
Art was inanimate and would never run
away
That man could caress the
Priceless skin of the canvas with his eyes
He could stare for hours and hours and the
painting would not shout or say:
'Sod off and leave me alone'
This was the seduction of art
This was why she was there,
To be close to the soul of a man she would
never know
To almost touch the fragile skin of canvases
and speak to them
Or listen to what they had to say.
The next day she went to the Francis Bacon
exhibition,
A spectacle within itself
'Was he a genius, now that his work sold for
tens of millions?'
The canvases were violent,

Dark generous globs of paint weaved into
complex patterns
That became faces,
Flesh that was painted as disease,
Enclosed rooms that became cells,
And all the while the skinny one thought of
Bacon's sharp tongue and generous heart,
His propensity to drink and his incredible
discipline.
The chaos of his studio that formed the
food for his art
And the incubator of pain
Setting the stage for
The violence of the brush stroke.
She remembered seeing her first Bacon
painting
Like no other painting she had ever seen
before with its rectangle of black
The permanent cage for the contorted,
tortured figure
That was on the verge of death or some
terrible deed
And the lone light bulb dangling from the
ceiling
That didn't radiate any light apart from
casting a shadow
That was hellish.
She walked into another room
Noticed that it was surprisingly sparse
And then she saw him
The smelly old man with cheeks that were
hollow
And the bulbous nose;
He peered eagerly at every picture
Left his finger prints on each glass cabinet

As he shuffled along he left
His sour onion scent on everything he
touched.
They locked eyes again, but although she
recognised him,
He didn't recognise her
She felt an instant connection to this man
who was seeking refuge in art -
A substitute for God and religion.
She hid behind her stylish mask; he wore
his soul on the outside
For everyone to see and reject
That smelly old man was
A vagabond, a misfit, an outcast that had
no place,
Drifting, just like she was.
That smelly old man was born a baby, with
pillow soft skin
Maybe he was cuddled and stroked by a
doting young mother, with high hopes for
her son.
But if the mother had foreseen what he
Would become it is entirely plausible that
she might have
Left him on the street in a bin liner to slowly
suffocate and die.
The mirror reflection of the putrid interior
soul
The morose, pathetic face of that smelly old
man would live in the underbelly of her
subconscious
Casting a deeper dent than a Bacon
painting ever could.

The Blue Elephant

The blue elephant lived by the sea in an
Old stone house with shutters
And a charm that was ancient,
A lonely girl saw the elephant sitting there
proudly
And put it in her pocket
Without even thinking.
Plucked from its home
The elephant was kidnapped
And protested loudly,
Trapped in that black, claustrophobic pocket
The elephant missed its view of the ocean
And began to cry
Why did the lonely girl steal that elephant?
Knowing that it was wrong.
She stole it
Because that elephant exuded something,
Something that cannot really be described
It was tiny, crafted with care and precision
Possessing an elegance and beauty.
It was a gift
A precious unfathomable gift,
But it was destined for greatness
To be immortalised in paintings
To be worshipped for its serenity.
That elephant was going to guide her
Teach her
Be her friend for life
As her hand followed the contours of its
back, trunk and dainty feet, she felt
vindicated.
The blue elephant stood bravely next to a
giant bone that threatened to crush it

Dented

While frenzied ants scurried, the blue
creature remained serene
Glowing in the sunlight
Not phased by the giant crevices in the
table
That could spell instant death if the
elephant inched any closer.
The splinters that jutted out the table did
not disturb the elephant
The elephant would stay eternally young
and smooth
Remain a shade of blue that almost glowed
in the dark
Under the stars
Now the elephant sat on a glass table in
London
Far away from its home in Messina
Missing the lullaby song of the sea
The elephant looked pitiful and meek
Disorientated like a monkey kidnapped from
the jungle and placed in a zoo.
The elephant waited,
Waited for the promise
Of being immortalised in paint but
There was no point painting it since
The elephant was perfect as it was,
A brush stroke would never capture its
essence,
Not even come close.
The blue of its skin grew dull and dusty
The scratches became all too apparent
It became just another thing
Just another object
Random paraphernalia
Junk that might one day be

Thrown away
Without a care or a thought,
Dumped unceremoniously in the Messina
Sea

Mental

'Don't go all mental'
Mental, but I am mentally unsound
It says as much in my medical records
They don't 'get it'
How can they?
For these last months it feels as though
I have been carrying two boulders
On my shoulders
With a brick pressing down upon my brain
Breathing air like mud
Struggling to inch forward
When I remain in the same spot
Sewn to this infested piece of ground
My creativity at a halt
I lie, preferring to sleep
This affliction robs me of everything
It steals the seconds, the minutes, the
hours
The germs that breed
Silently on a polished surface
Are multiplying in my head.
Eggs are laid on clean white sheets
By millions of greedy little bugs
And they crawl all over you in your sleep.
You can't see the mental cancer as it
spreads
As your brain succumbs day by day
Eaten on the inside
And then slowly your eyes
Look like they've been scooped out
And you're blind
What time is it?
Do not know or care

When you think you have nothing left
The fresh weight
That grows heavier
Pressing upon your bones
Melts like snow
And you are bare again
Naked and shivering in the cold

Nearly died

It had grown into an Amazonian green
monster of a beauty
Over the years, a few inches longer like a
greedy snake
Leaves unfurling reaching out for the sun
It looked like a waterfall in full flow
A stream travelling up her staircase
And so she re-positioned it
Perched at the top of her bookshelf,
To allow its bushy green mane to cascade
freely,
To dance in the light and soak up the
goodness of those morning rays.
For years just a drop of water each week
A feel of the soil
Only a little was required
Now the green specimen was far from her
reach
A ladder was necessary
More effort needed to feed it
And sometimes she would forget
Two weeks passed without a drink and the
leaves started to droop
Alarm set in when she the plant was dying
Then panic and desperation ensued
She flooded the plant with a full jug of
water
The equivalent of a mini ocean.
The surplus water gushed like a tsunami
Drenching her books
Leaving a splattering of soil on her
Shiny sisal carpet.
The plant was not revived

The leaves grew droopier
Limp like a disinterested penis
The tiny leaves with that delectable coating
of fur began to shrivel
What to do?
The plant was removed from its perch
Lifted out of its pot
The stink of brown, filthy water was rank
A slow drink of poison
A methodical drowning
An inevitable rotting of the roots
The water was promptly washed away,
The pot rinsed clean
The leaves showered with water that was
fresh and pure
And then the plant was deposited back on
its perch
Accompanied with a daily prayer,
'Please live, don't die, you don't know how
much pleasure I have gleaned from the
sprouting of a new leaf and the flow of your
verdant mane.'
Leaves continued to dry up and wither
Five here, ten there, even more
Each night a futile prayer
Each day the hope dwindled
But then as leaves died new ones slowly
began to grow
Tiny leaves with fresh fur and the bloom of
youth
Fighting and gasping for life and light
A gentle stroke with human fingertips
A low hum and the exchange of a few
words of encouragement
And the weakened specimen began to

revive
With a steady determination.

For new life to grow, the old must depart to
another place
The inevitable cycle of life and death
continued
From the sunny perch of a bookshelf.

What nearly died
Somehow
Managed to renew and live on
Such is the mystery of life.

Where Ever I Go

Where ever I go
Who ever I am with
Will always carry you with me
Gave you my heart
And then you smashed it into
A thousand pieces
You laughed when I said this
While inside I cried.
No more tears
Only big smiles
I must turn this love for you into
Something meaningful
Even if it means a life without you
Remember the boy that you once were
The one who read philosophy
Who ruminated on the meaning of life
The one who loved to submerge his mind in
mathematics
Who likes trees and taking long walks with
your dog, Jack
Remember that boy
Don't let that boy die
Because he was the boy I fell in love with
All those years ago
But what has become of you now
All your hair has gone
Replaced with a head that seems ginormous
Your face drawn
You have millions in the bank
But you seem lonely and lost
Your eyes glare
Your nostrils flare imperiously
The boy in you died

The man that you have become
Is someone else
Whom I could never love
I mourn that boy
Knowing you killed him with ambition
Has he gone forever?
No, I still remember him fondly
He resides within me
But with each passing day
The memory dwindles
And slowly dies
Until it is dust

Baby P

Baby P
What is your name?
When I saw your face,
Your bright blue eyes,
Golden blond curls
The promise in those cherubic cheeks
Were you looking up at your mother or
father?
You were smiling then
That's what they used to call you
'Smiley'
Then I saw that last photo of you
Your face smeared in chocolate,
Your finger pressed to your lips,
Your eyes bigger and wider and sadder,
How sad your eyes were,
Your golden curls shaved off,
There were fifty wounds and scabs on your
tiny body
Or so they say?
Your body weight had plummeted
Sometimes your hunger forced you to eat
soil or
The discarded biscuits of other kids.
Pus oozed from your torn off ear
And bashed up head
Two fingernails ripped off with pliers
The tip of your finger sliced off.
They say that your mother's boyfriend
Used to skin frog's alive and break their legs
for kicks
Now he had a human to experiment on.
Fascinated with Hitler he was

Afflicted with a multitude of mental health
problems
Or perhaps simply a sadist.
While your mother played poker
Or watched porn
She let him 'look after you'
Spinning you from the top of a chair
Until you fell off
She was crazy in love
You were a worthy sacrifice to keep her
man
He bashed you gleefully from your ankles
onto the floor
And when you cried he just threw you in
the cot to let you
Decompose and congeal.
In that final image of you
Baby P
You looked like you wanted to die
As if you had endured enough of life
During your barely there seventeen months
These adult protectors all discussed you at
length
Prodding and
Checking you
The pediatrician who didn't notice your
broken ribs or broken back
Who said you were too 'cranky and
miserable'
And therefore it was not possible to
examine you.
The overloaded social worker, duped by
your 'cooperative mother',
Unable to see beyond the chocolate
smothered all over your face

To conceal your bruises.
If I had seen you
On a London street in Haringey
Would I have recoiled in disgust at your
terrible state?
They say you were always dirty
Reeking of vomit and urine
Living in a house with faeces, dead animals,
Rottweiler's, rats and pornography
Would I have looked the other way?
Intimidated by your overweight mother and
her neo Nazi boyfriend.
And what of the lodger
What did he do to you baby P?
If I had known you I hope I would have
smiled
Bounced you on my knee
Played with you until you giggled
Patted your back and cradled you to sleep
I would never have wanted to hurt you
Only cuddle and cherish you
Baby P,
But parents can be cruel
I know that only too well
You are small
Adults are big
They have power
You must submit
What choice do you have?
Does any child have a choice?
When an adult is triggered and
Morphs into a monster who screams
Calls you a 'fucking idiot' and
Doesn't hesitate to punch you.
The fact that you're a baby

Makes you easy bait
For bullies, psychopaths and the rest
Even the ones you would never suspect
Now a whole nation mourns you.
A child dies each week
At the hands of parents, care givers and
relatives
Right now a child is being tortured
Starved, beaten, raped
Humiliated, yelled at and smacked.
Why did she bother to have you Baby P?
Only to neglect and toss you to the dogs
Her boyfriend said, 'I never meant to kill
him, I was just trying to toughen him up'.
The night before your death you received a
blow so hard that you swallowed your
tooth,
The police found you under a blanket of
your own blood,
It was hard to see the bruises because you
were cold and blue,
Dead for some time before they discovered
you.

Why do people have children?
When they are simply intent on killing
Tormenting
Humiliating
And belittling them.

Are they simply repeating the
Tired, sad patterns of childhood
Did they simply not know any better?

If any of us could choose

Would we honestly choose the parents that
bore us?

You were one of 200 at risk in Haringey
And three million in Britain
Maybe 100 million in the world -
Probably more.
Children like you are
Treated worse than rubbish
Except rubbish can be recycled
Transformed into something brand new.
If someone had loved, cared and fed you
Where would you be now?
At least now you are sleeping
At peace somewhere

Enfeebled by this case
Powerless to do anything
Only silent outrage leaks
These words are for you Baby P
I won't ever forget you.

Where The Heck Are You?

'Where the heck are you?'
A distant ex-lover asks
'Well I live in a modest house with worn
wooden floors
Perched precariously on a hill
And I sit in a room with a view of the ocean
and far off mountains.
Occasionally a bird flies into my room
Perched on the corner of my table and
quietly watches me paint,
But when she starts to chirp I shoo her off.

Am far away from anyone or anything,
Don't need clothes or material things,
Don't even need this computer
Although it is easier for me to write on it,
So that's how I justify having it.'

'Where the heck are you?'
A curious friend asks
'Well I live in a cave at the bottom of the
ocean and sleep next to
An amiable whale
At night I listen to his whale song and take
a stroll in his belly,
Befriend other fish and a pink octopus,
Eat seaweed and then spit it out in disgust.

Am far away from anyone or anything
I don't need human company,
Idle chitchat.
Don't even need to make love anymore

Although I never thought I would ever say
that before.'

'Where the heck are you?
Was just thinking where you could be,
It's so 1930's to mysteriously disappear.'
'Actually, I have gone back in time
Living the life described in an F. Scott.
Fitzgerald novel
The Damned and the Beautiful, how fucking
corny?
Drinking champagne and smoking long
elegant cigarettes
Tomorrow I might visit the 1600s
Or maybe race into the future
To zoom about in spaceships and sip tea on
the moon
Or drive a racing car like Senna.

Am far away from anyone or anything,
Don't need to party, to dress up in stylish
rags and look desirable,
Don't need to indulge in adventures and
escapades,
Quite happy to be still'.

'Where the heck are you?
Why don't you just say instead of
Couching your whereabouts in such
Cloak and dagger mystery?'
'Well if I really told you where I was,
Inhabiting a grey and eerily quiet
landscape,
You might try to lure me back
Would rather say I am living in my head

Dented

Plucking out paintings that I talked about
Arranging poems from jumbled up words
Drawing things that unravel and flow like
water.
To live in my mind and fly on the wings of a
child's imagination
Is to be wherever the hell I want to be
For everyday to be a new piece of paper
A new canvas
To puncture the silence with the sound I
want to fill it with
To paint on the white canvas what I want to
paint
To draw on the paper what I see clearly
This is the answer to your incessant
questioning
Are you satiated now?
Is the mystery over?
Do you pity me for settling for grey
Instead of
Ultramarine Yves Klein pigment blue?
Or do you see it was the only way for me to
Unshackle a captive mind and
Inch towards luminous liberty
And finally be rid of you.'

Sense

Cannot make sense of your death
The last time I saw you was exactly two
years ago
It sounds hideously glib, but I never got to
say good-bye
Not in the way that I wanted to.
The last time you saw me, I was haggard,
distressed, and sick
It pains me to think that this is your final
memory
Of what I had become rather than the
person I used to be
Not the picture I wanted you to remember
Will never know what you really ever
thought
As the days became months and then years
Never believed I would give up on you,
But I suppose I did
Give up.
This last week I haven't cried a tear
Your memory appears like a favourite flower
And then withers almost instantaneously
'You were infatuated,' a no-nonsense friend
reminded me
It didn't feel like infatuation
Never really bothered you
Or inundated you with letters or calls
No one ever knew the depth of my feelings
Not even you
Seldom imposed or demanded
Preferred to conceal my feelings with
A flimsy sobriety
Apart from that one time

Dented

When I begged you to stop snorting the
white worm.
That fiendish white worm
How I loathed it
How I wanted to
Banish it completely from your life,
But it was your life to trash
Your choice entirely
So, I remained a useless bystander
As you pressed
Self-destruct
And for what
A silly, vacuous blond girl
Who broke your heart
And went off with your best friend.
For hours I listened to your torment
Was there for you
As you were for me
I loved you
What if that one night when you seduced
me
What if I had let you inside me?
Without protection,
Which is what you insisted upon
As I adamantly refused
And what if you had come
And a baby followed with your greenish
blue eyes.
Would that child have made you stop
feeding off the white worm?
Would that child have made you love me?
You are in another place
Wish I could be with you
Perhaps the same place as my dead dad
He was our age when he died

Maybe you are having a cigarette and a
drink with him
Telling him all about the daughter, your
doting friend,
He never got to know
Laughing up there or down there.
Life is lonely without you
It was lonelier with you
Knowing you were roaming the world,
But I couldn't reach you
Now I can talk to you
I think you are listening
Gatecrashing my dreams
And they become more real
Than any stale reality.
Life is a loveless one
One without touch
Without intimacy
Without the promise of an orgasm
Or any disappointment
Since I no longer yearn or feel anything
much,
Apart from the rectangular battlegrounds
that start off white
The ones that I scream at,
Batter with my fists and stare at for hours
without blinking,
The ones that I loathe and love
Because they are all I have.
And the memory that is what you once
were
And what you have become in my head
How many dialogues will I have with you?
Conversations where no one utters a sound
Will scratch and pick with my fingers

Trying to scrape an inkling of meaning from
somewhere.
But as the seconds slip through my hands
With my faded youth clenched in both fists
I die a little
Waiting to join you.
Wishing I had died before you to save your
mother the torment
Would you be crying over me as I have
cried over you?
Would you never forget me as I will never
forget you?
It makes no sense that you are gone
You were not supposed to go first
It was I
Dearest one
Adam
I miss you, man.

Saira = Raisa

Her friend was near and the skinny one
didn't know why
But she wanted to show him something
A tiny note written by her mother
The second letter that she received
Which she cherished like a precious
painting.
She'd never felt her mother's love before
Only her wrath
Now her mother described the skinny one
as a 'golden thread'
A thread that weaved golden tapestries
Tapestries that lit up the world
'I love you'
Her mother simply wrote in the second
letter
On the tiniest piece of paper
Her handwriting child like and elegant.
The skinny one cried and kept it safe in her
golden treasure chest of precious things
Then she pulled out a small post-it note
drawn by Saira
Of two girls with large smiles, one big and
one little and the words
'Sisters' written in a child's hand
Then she saw a photo
The skinny one was holding the little girl
that was Saira
She was two at the time
Wearing a red school jumper and a nappy
Her hair a spray of dark silky curls
Her cheeks like creamy snow
A smile so pure it made you gooey inside

And light up to see it
The skinny one was holding the child as if
she never wanted to let go
Holding her
Close
Ever so close
Cheek to cheek
And in this photo she was no longer skinny,
But plump and bright
Her cheeks the same colour as the little one
And she held her tight as the child laughed
with delight
She remembered that those were the years
where
Nothing mattered
Only art and Saira.
Saira gave her the love that she had been
seeking
Saira was the food that nourished her soul
Saira was the one who at aged three
refused to kill a spider
The skinny one instinctively stuck out her
foot to flatten the mortified creature,
But Saira scooped it up with gentle, tiny
hands and set it free in the grass
'Don't be scared,' she said and the skinny
one was stunned by her wisdom
Saira taught her how to love
Saira nourished her with giggles
Saira was all she needed
At sixteen the skinny one was reborn
With the birth of her little sister,
But then at nineteen the skinny one went
away
To a big, bad, dirty, glorious

Beast of a city
When all she wanted to do was paint in her
bedroom and play with Saira.
One night the giant hand of London
grabbed her by the scruff of her wiry neck
And planted her
Far away from Saira
And she forgot how to love
She forgot
For sixteen years
Until she found the picture of the two of
them
Sisters
Locked in a rare embrace
And then she remembered what they once
had,
But soon forgot again
For the love was nowhere to be found

The Unadulterated Man

There was a man called Pieter
He told her he was Dutch
From the land of her favourite painter
Dearest troubled Vincent, except Pieter was
a trader.
Obscenely rich, according to him
The skinny one dismissed him in an instant
Wrongly so, she openly admitted later
She wondered what he thought of her
In her black rubber dress and shiny high
heels
An artist masquerading as a diva - or a slut?
But then he sat down beside her
Told her how much he liked her red coat
Read the skinny one's humble book
He looked at each page and said, 'This is
deep'.
He related to the clouds and trees
Because he lived on top of a mountain
Where often he would sit and watch the sky
Dreaming of living there amongst the clouds
like she did.
As they talked
Pieter suddenly asked her, 'Are you happy?'
She thought long before replying
That night she was unmoved by the sight of
Naked limbs and flesh
Interlocked in a glib orgy at 33 Portland
Place
Rather she was happy to have a
Gentle conversation with a
Gentle being and left content
With a warmth that stirred her tired soul

Content to have a genuine conversation.
She penned a few words in her sketchbook
The window to her heart
Penned a poem for Pieter
'I am honoured,' he said
And she was happy to make someone
smile.
'What's that?' he asked pointing at her shiny
helmet
'Oh it's for my spaceship,' and then she took
off in seconds
Racing through the London streets
With music tingling in her ears.
What determines the collision
Of random souls in the universe?
What determines the formation of the
clouds in the sky?
What makes a mountain?
What makes a man decent and kind?
What makes a man respect a woman?
What makes a man good?
When all she encounters are little pricks
Who think they have big dicks
Can they not accept that the skinny one
Has the biggest cock in the universe?
Is that why men try and crush
Belittle, *Kick*, *Trample*, *Spit*
On her and treat her like a
Bitch?
'I am no bitch, I respect man, animal and
the universe.'
But she is yet to meet an unadulterated
man.
Does such a man exist?

Stink

Here no one saw her
Here it didn't matter to be alluring
Here she was invisible
Everyday the same clothes
Everyday her face bare
Everyday when she looked at her reflection
She felt ill
'Hag,' that's what her husband said
And that's what she looked like
A hag
A stinking, rotten hag
Her skin unwashed
Her hair greasy
Her clothes were beginning to pong from
stale body odour
Paint was embedded under her nails
'No one will touch me now,'
She was making herself physically repulsive
Something she'd been doing
Consistently as a child
Why?
She knew why
All that mattered was to become so
repulsive that any sexual desire died
Because why would anyone want to touch
An ageing, mad, old hag?
That old woman walking the streets
Shoving her bags along the pavement
Shuffling her soggy, pink slippered feet
Back hunched
Face weathered and beaten like an old, torn
umbrella

That had battled too many storms in a
lifetime
'It doesn't matter what I look like when I
will end up looking like her'
She was referring to a recently completed
portrait
Of an old Bangladeshi lady,
Probably dead by now,
Her eyes were two loveless caves
Her mouth frozen in a pursed, subtle scowl
She was waiting for death
Waiting for a bleak end
Each wrinkle on her face was loaded with
The heavy burden of melancholy
'When was the last time someone dared to
hold her in their arms?
Thirty years, forty years
Her pussy had sealed up and she was a
chaste again
Dressed in a white sari like a mournful, pure
angel.
She recalled her years as a teenage slob
Not bothering
Not caring
Not washing for days
Seeing how long her stink would go
unnoticed.
You know kids who
Deliberately
Eschew all personal hygiene
Kids who make themselves physically
repulsive
It's a familiar sign
Of being abused
Sexually, emotionally, physically

Dented

Not slothfulness
They feel dirty
So they become the filth
That is all they see
When they look in the mirror.

When this skinny, gauche girl turned fifteen
She was noticed by the world
'You should be a model,' they all cooed
And the self-conscious
Reluctant grooming began
The painting of the face
The vertiginous heels
The styling of the hair
The arrangement of the clothes
The photo shoots, the fuss, the vain
nonsense of it all,
But it was all a sham
A stupid charade
Another mask

She would always regress to that teenage
phase of
Slobbishness
Of being totally indifferent
Of being repelled by her body
Of being blind to the opposite sex
Of eschewing all touch
Of only wanting to touch her mind with
knowledge
Or taint her fingers with paint.
She was invisible at last
An ugly
Stinking
Creature

Without child
Only the baggage of life
With its foul odour
Reminding her of the past
To be called a 'hag' didn't offend
It only confirmed what she was
That without the paint, the clothes, the
effort
When stripped bare of the careful
camouflage
The sight was ghastly and hideous.
'I am redundant, my exterior is rotting, but
what I write, what I say, what I think, what
I draw, what I paint, the music I compose
can be...
Pure, enduring and edifying.'
The past will always haunt
It can't be shifted
Hence she is forced to carry the heavy
shadow of seemingly forgotten truths,
Night and day;
Yet it is the possibility to move,
To make someone cry, to laugh, to see the
world differently
To dazzle, to confront, to confound
That makes life meaningful.
This surface that is diseased
Is not worth preserving
Why waste all that time washing,
deodorising and smothering
The natural gross smell that we would all
exude if we were stranded on a desert
island
Devoid of our taps,
Showers and soap?

Dented

To stink was a sudden emancipation
From the persistent torment of trying to be
Stunning, perfect and polished clean
When she knew she was forever dirty
Because of what had happened
In her childhood past
'I want to simply be real
To think
To be
And to...
Stink.'

Shining Light

He was tall with bright eyes that dazzled
when he smiled
Dynamic and dashing when he donned a
suit
He would slide on the dance floor lost in the
beats
Stroke the wheel of the car as he flew
through the air
Rip up the roads on his bike
Sail the Thai ocean in his boat and climb a
mountain
Just to meditate
He read books about spirituality to cleanse
his mind
He called you up when you were sad
Tried to take the ache away with a joke and
a hug
Made the best smoked salmon and
scrambled eggs on toast
He would praise enthusiastically,
The superlatives would trip off the tongue
He loved his dogs, how he loved them,
Especially the noble, elegant Hercules
And his beloved mother.
He was always talking about her
He was there to protect his 'angel' mother,
Didn't want anything to hurt her
He kept the photo of the two of them for
everyone to see,
A woman with flowing blond hair cradling a
beautiful boy in her arms.
When he grew up he became restless,
Desperate to build something with his own

two hands,
Something he could call his own.
He was a shy artist,
A humble philosopher
Curious about life, curious about people
He had an abundance of love flowing
through his veins
His eyes
His smile
His laughter
His beauty was within and without
He shone too bright for this world
Burning slowly
And yes there were times
He could be callous and selfish
Played games
Pulled towards only to push away
Slightly narcissistic,
Slightly spoilt
Slightly smug.
Some dismissed you
Others derided
But now that you are gone
None of it matters
Who is even close to perfect?
Oh shining, fractured light
Shine on

Easier

'It is easier to be silent' she thought, it is
easier not to care
She tried not to, but her heart was
screaming out for something
He said he would call her back for two days
now
He did not.
No explanation, every hour or so she stared
at her phone
Thinking perhaps he's busy,
Tired,
Or fallen for another.
Night came and the agony did not stop
As thoughts crashed through flimsy mental
barriers.
He's only human, the age gap between
them seemed like a
Huge and unbridgeable chasm
Such indifference hurt,
Her pride stopped her from calling
'This wretched pattern must stop,' she
demanded
She put everything on the line to keep this
putrid corpse alive
When she really ought to end the nonsense
That was this tattered relationship
They were death to one another
Death
She knew it and yet couldn't keep away.
The inanity of infatuation
Such a source of ruination
Yes this infatuation had ruined her life
She let it

Dented

Love is a disease of the mind
'Enough,' she said
Love can kill
Slowly
Yet she never once tried to stop it
Stoked the flames
In fact, and let it burn furiously
Contaminated by the putrefaction of a
fantasy that
Made her digress from the
Right path,
Whatever that is?
Long, long ago
Why?
What was the source of this infatuation?
What was the attraction of unrequited love?
Was she addicted to the rejection?
The constant feeling of being alone
The constant frustration tinged with a hint
of bitterness
The constant hankering for something that
he stopped giving eons ago
What was the source of these misguided
emotions?
Such entangled, stupid emotions that made
her restless
Disturbed her sleep when she was tired
Disturbed her when awake
Made her want to roar and tear out her
heart
With her teeth
Made her want to disappear.
She had been wading in the deep murky
sea,
Drifting for years,

Reaching out for a distant hand that
Seemed to wave to her in the shadows,
But it was just that
Shadows
Deriding her with insidious laughter
As she groped and cried out to
Nothingness
That was velvety and soft
Scary and cold
Vast and eerie.
The darkness was all she knew
The voices and visions bored her now,
She wanted to banish them
She wanted to hold another
To engage in conversation
To laugh even
To feel the skin of someone against hers
And banish this sick love that plagued
The darkness was persistently loyal
The darkness refused to leave
Perhaps that was why he was silent?
And retreated after seven years of
Groping in the mud
Trudging through the emotional morass
with a sallow face
And a callowness of feeling.
This dead love affair grew weary at his feet
He kicked it away spitefully
Did he still have her photos in his bedroom?
Propped up against the wall, not yet hung
If ever
Maybe it was easier to have them lying
around
Easier to throw them in a cupboard when
she was not looking

Dented

It was easier to say the love was dead
And her soul dead, too
Everything was moribund
With a neat and drab finality
Apart from the pen that she took for a walk
Each day twitching tirelessly
Stabbing the flimsy surface of the paper
with the nib,
It was simply easier to stab than to love

Wish We'd Never Met

Thoroughly enjoyed the first film I ever saw
you in
Was dazzled in fact
By your voice and your face
Wish I had left it at that
Until you caught my eye at a private
members club.
Was dressed as Mia
My glamorous alter ego
Hiding behind her stunning mask
Donning a striking orange dress
You'd noticed me apparently
Drawing in my sketchbook at the dinner
table
As I tried to avoid my ex-lover.
We spoke
You asked for my number
Rather audaciously,
And feigned diffidence
Didn't ask for yours
'Why do you want my number?'
I should have asked, 'You barely know me.'
Still, you were pleasant and charming
Why didn't I just walk away?
People like me
Don't mix with your sort.

That's how I was before
Indifferent
To the rich and famous
Thought they were a sad bunch
The vast majority
Chasing something

Dented

That didn't exist.

I was sauntering home one day
In Manchester
Lost in thought
When Jason from *Take That,*
Have you heard of the band?
Pulled up in his vintage car
And promptly got out
He stood, stared and grinned
Expecting me to get in, I presume
The sheer bloody cheek
Didn't say a word
My wide-eyed expression of horror must
have said it all
Then he drove away,
Slapped on the face by rejection
Maybe he was used to over zealous girls
spreading their legs with predictable zeal?

That's the way to always be
Not overawed
Ever
By anyone
Because man is feeble and mortal
And ever so weak.

Not sure why I had a book of poems with
me that night
Poems I had penned and published in 2007
It was an exercise I had done
To great effect before in New York and
London
Getting others to read my work

Except I chose the wrong poem that fateful
night:
An ode to love and lust
With references to an anus, cock and pussy.
Actually it wasn't smutty
It was very profound
The story of how lustful passion
Is a poor substitute for sustaining love.
He read it in front of his friends
Who were playing scrabble,
He just didn't get it
The meaning of my humble poem.

He was an actor
Not a scholar

The sudden change in his expression
As if I was dirt
Was mortifying
He abruptly escorted me out of the building
There was an awkward goodbye as the lift
doors closed shut
And I wondered how it could have gone
Just so terribly wrong
In the space of minutes.

Saw him again a few months later
Was sitting with my friend Yinka, an artist,
Quite a respected one,
Whom he didn't recognise.
He acted as if I was an irritation
My number probably deleted by now on his
A-list phone
Crammed with far more worthy people.
Then he won an Oscar,

Dented

For a performance that was universally
acclaimed
Saw his smug mug everywhere
Couldn't escape that pretty boy face of his.
He got married to someone very suitable
and compatible
With pale skin and long wavy hair
They had a baby
His career soared

My mental health crumbled

The year I met him was 2009
A few months later I had psychosis
And during that psychotic narrative,
Which almost fried my brain,
I was the chosen one
The star of my own story
The ruler in a parallel universe.
As he ascended and became immortal
Like a god
I remained in the gutter
A worm in the mud
Except I couldn't see the stars
Only their pointed edges sliced
A mind already torn to pieces
That lay lost in the desert.
There are many days I cannot get out of
bed
Or brush my teeth
Or work
Can barely manage an hour of
concentration
Cannot get dressed or wash or eat
My mind is haunted

By memories that are redundant
But remain sharp and cut.
These faces,
Including his,
Continue to taunt from the screen
Or leer from giant billboards
As others swoon and gush at the sheer
sight of them
Long, instead, to gouge out my eyes
In order to no longer see their perfect
airbrushed faces
And instead find meaning
In a life that has become meaningless.
He has long forgotten the encounter,
But not I
The humiliation as palpable and brutal
As it was on that first night
My god, I wish we'd never met
Mr Redmayne.

Bombs

The bombs are raining down as she writes,
Blood and dirt cakes the faces of baffled
children
Too afraid to sleep as they lay awake
Their belongings hiding under a blanket of
broken concrete
People scour for remnants of their life with
bleeding hands
Protests continue around the world
A spate of new suicide bombers is born
The economy is collapsing
Fortunes shrinking or simply gone over
night
House prices are plummeting
Billionaire's are slitting their wrists
And the precious objects that we covet are
blown to bits.
The forecasts are depressing
Nothing is what it seems
Now family is the most important thing
To cherish and hold on to
Even that is not for sure
Family can have jagged edges
Family can be obliterated in seconds.
As another baby is abused, possibly
murdered
In their own home, and stuffed in a suitcase
Fathers lock their kids in dank cellars
Impregnate their daughters
And terrorise their wives or the other way
round
People can't drink a clean glass of water
Flush a toilet

Wash their hands
Take a shower
They die of cholera and the flies swarm and
feast
On their skeletal corpses
With green bulbous eyes
As photographers take their snaps eagerly
And broadcast them around the world.
These are the wars we hear about
The bombings
The neglect
The abuse
The pillage
And what of the silent war
That is persistently taking place in the
skinny one's head
'You have nothing to cry about, you have
beauty, intelligence, money and talent'
That's what they all retort, glibly
Yet conflict has been seething for decades
The shells pulverise, stamping out the light
The rubble gathers heavily in a war torn
mind
The red rust of memories
Of lost dreams and hopes
The disease that comes from dirty water
Has permeated every inch of her being
Her flesh is viscous and flies feed discreetly
From her open wounds
The abuse is unremittingly profuse
That dark mysterious voice ordering her to
end it all
And hang from the hook
She sees jutting out
Of an imposing black wooden door;

Dented

Her weary head bombarded with a barrage
of images
And a fastidious plan where no detail is
overlooked.

The bombs rain down everywhere
Internally
Externally
There is the devastation that we can see
That we hear about
That is disgustingly palpable and tangible
There are the sick stories that the press
love to relay
The stories of betrayal, depravity and
torture
The stories that rescind the myth of 'family'
There are the images of the developing
world
The cracked layers of poverty and
corruption
Poisoning the people and stopping them
from breathing
An air that seems permanently polluted.
There are the alarmist headlines of
economic doom and gloom
That will lead to widespread unemployment,
homelessness, closures,
Depression and suicide while the select few
live in
Luxury with money they gleefully flaunt and
burn at parties,
But will never manage to spend in their
lifetime,
What will they do with their billions?
Take it all to their grave

While the banks fervently print more of the
stuff
In order for people to consume more things
they can't afford or need
And the silent wars continue
The one's in your head
Burn.

The bombs rain down
And the world continues to whir
Wheezing heavily like a heavy smoker
Will it one day stop?
'We are born... we do what we can... we
die... and that's it,'
Francis Bacon said cheerily, 'I am positive
about nothing,' he added with a chuckle
He got rid of his despair through painting
While drinking with a smile in *The Colony
Rooms*
Mr Bacon had the last laugh
Perhaps he numbed the pain with alcohol
Losing himself in the dance of paint
Catching the random depraved accident
with both fists
Blasting it violently on the canvas that was
his second home
A home he sometimes trashed
And occasionally shat in,
But always in the end he dismissed
Everything
To free himself of attachment to anything
Or a notion that might suggest
An erroneous idea of peace or stability.

The horror would remain

Dented

In the room
As he laughed in an inebriated stupor
And heads rolled like footballs.
As she raises her brush she can't ignore this
horror
That the world tolerates and accepts
She can't be so indifferent
Can't laugh at another senseless
decapitation
Only get fired up and angry as
She hears those stupid gunshots
Petrifyingly loud.
The intractable conflicts continue with an
insidious sneer,
There is no end
As another tyrannical buffoon
Is elected President.
Dictators party while their subjects starve
And immigrants go underground
Huddling in dark corners
Where they can no longer be seen or heard.

Blood is everywhere
Leaking through the perforated dots
Peppering her translucent skin
1000s of them like
A Kusama painting
That has gone insane

Man craves war more than life
Sucking the bombs lovingly like
Caramel toffees
That tick tock
Waiting to explode
In our tiny faces

'I want the bombs to stop raining,' she cries
out in her sleep,
But they don't
And she knows they never will.

Photo courtesy of Laurence Edney

Artist, writer and filmmaker Sanchita Islam has worked extensively in the Tower Hamlets region since 1999 and has participated widely in exhibitions and screenings, working with the elderly, women suffering from domestic violence, kids living in the slums of Bangladesh, street kids in Jakarta, kids living on the estates of east London and Kuala Lumpur and most recently patients with mental health problems in Brussels and Malaysia.

Islam completed her BSc (econ) and MSc (econ) at the London School of Economics before embarking on a Channel 4 sponsored MA at the Northern Media School in Directing and Screenwriting, and a BA in the Practice and Theory of Visual Art at Chelsea School of Art and Design. She dropped out in her second year and set up Pigment Explosion in 1999. She has produced and directed fifteen films to date including shorts and one-hour films and exhibited and screened her films in London, Brussels, New York, Paris, Bangladesh, Jakarta, Kuala Lumpur, Rome, India, Pakistan, Frankfurt and Yangon. She is currently working of a feature film trilogy *Portrait of Madness*. She has shown at the Whitechapel, ICA and Hayward Gallery and completed over 100 group/solo shows and screenings of her films including the show *Schizophrenia Part 1* where she showed as four artists at the Truman Brewery in 2007. She was artist in resident at the Whitechapel Art Gallery and artist in resident at Open Gallery and Shoreditch House, Her art has featured in various venues around London such as Shoreditch House, Mark Hix's restaurants, and the Clifton Hotel Group in Bristol. The Arts Council, BBC and British Council have funded her films and five books. These include *From Briarwood to Barishal to Brick Lane*, *Old Meets Young*, *Hidden*, *Connecting Kids* and *Avenues*. Pigment Explosion branched out into book publication producing its first publication *The Cloud Catcher*. Chipmunka Publishing published her first volume of poems *Eternal Pollution of a Dented Mind* and her novel *Gungi Blues* in 2008. The theatre group ESTACA ZERO TEATRO in Portugal performed her two plays, *The Suitcase* and *Hello*. In 2010 the UK Film Council commissioned the animation film *White Wall*.

Islam had a mid-career retrospective at Rich Mix in March 2013. Brussels based art organisation vzw KAOS and the Psycho-Social Centre St-Alexius awarded her a grant to complete a second scroll project with patients suffering from mental health problems in Brussels 2014. Rich Mix invited Pigment Explosion to exhibit this second scroll and perform her play *Do I Look Like a Fucking Mad Person?* in June 2015. The Arts Council and British Council awarded her an *Artist International Development Fund* grant in 2014 to complete a new scroll project in Bangladesh and Burma. In January 2015 she screened her film *White Wall* at the *Dhaka International Film Festival* and in March 2015 she screened *White Wall* and read excerpts from her book at Pansodan Gallery in Yangon, Burma. Muswell Hill Press published her book, written under the pseudonym Q.S Lam *Schizophrenics Can Be Good Mothers Too*, in January 2015. The book was launched in London at Shoreditch House and Rich Mix in June 2015 and at Brick Lane Bookshop 2016. She exhibited her *War on a Scroll Part 1* created with patients suffering from mental health problems at KAOS, Brussels, 2016. She has spoken at the House of Lords and House of Commons about mental health. In conjunction with the *1001 First Critical Days* campaign, Sanchita's work featured in the landmark show *Tomorrow's Child*, which focused on the importance of maternal mental health on a baby's future mental well being. Oyez!, based in Kuala Lumpur, is publishing her first children's book, *The Tree People.* Her writing has also been published in the book *The Recovery Letters*, 2017 and *A Day in My Head*, 2017. She has also worked with the *Malaysian Mental Health Association,* completing her first scroll with mentally ill patients in Kuala Lumpur October 2016. Her work also featured in a

MMHA book publication *Living With Mental Disorders*, 2016. She was invited by Dr Ang from MMHA to speak in Singapore about mental health in October 2016 at the *Second Asia Pacific Conference on Mental Health*. In 2016 she launched her global mental health campaign *MentalHealth4All* to raise basic mental health awareness.

Islam branched out into music, starting in March 2016, after recalling memories of child sex abuse. She has produced over 100 tracks and 10 albums: *Pain = Alchemy = Transformation Part 1 – 10*, and has performed in Singapore, London and Berlin. She calls the genre *Mental Music*, all the music relates to mental pain.

In October 2017 she will be performing her first *Mental Music* event at Shoreditch House in October 2017, and exhibiting new artwork, including a Grenfell Tower triptych and performing new songs at Wilford X Gallery in Brussels, at the invitation of Brussels based psychiatrist and artist Dr Erik Thys.

Islam remains staunchly independent and has tried to create a buzz outside the contemporary art scene while keeping one big toe firmly in it. She writes a blog artmotherhoodandmadness@tumblr.com and also contributes for the Huffington Post writing about mental health, politics, social issues and motherhood.